THE PRACTICE OF PSYCHOANALYSIS

THE PRACTICE OF PSYCHOANALYSIS

Thierry Bokanowski

Translated by
David Alcorn

KARNAC
LONDON NEW YORK

First published in French *De la pratique analytique* in 1998 by
Presses Universitaires de France

First published in English in 2006 by
H. Karnac (Books) Ltd.
6 Pembroke Buildings, London NW10 6RE

Translated by David Alcorn, 2006

British Library Cataloguing in Publication Data

A C.I.P. for this book is available from the British Library

ISBN-10: 1 85575 389 8
ISBN-13: 978 1 85575 389 1

Edited, designed and produced by The Studio Publishing Services Ltd,
www.publishingservicesuk.co.uk
e-mail: studio@publishingservices.co.uk

Printed in Great Britain

10 9 8 7 6 5 4 3 2 1

www.karnacbooks.com

CONTENTS

ABOUT THE AUTHOR

Thierry Bokanowski is a training analyst of the Paris Psychoanalytical Society (SPP) and a member of the International Psychoanalytical Association. A former secretary of the executive committee of the Paris Psychoanalytical Institute and former editor of the *Revue Française de Psychanalyse*, he is the current President of the Scientific Committee of the Paris Psychoanalytical Society. Several of Thierry Bokanowski's papers have been published in the various psychoanalytical Journals, including the *International Journal of Psycho-Analysis*. His widely-acclaimed book on Sándor Ferenczi was published in 1997 by the Presses Universitaires de France and has been translated into several languages.

Introduction

> Analytic experience has taught us that the better is always the enemy of the good[1] and that in every phase of the patient's recovery we have to fight against his inertia, which is ready to be content with an incomplete solution [. . .]
>
> We should not reckon on meeting with a resistance against the uncovering of resistances [. . .] They are resistances not only to the making conscious of contents of the id, but also to the analysis as a whole, and thus to recovery.
>
> Here let us pause for a moment to assure the analyst that he has our sincere sympathy in the very exacting demands he has to fulfil in carrying out his activities. It almost looks as if analysis were the third of those "impossible" professions in which one can be sure beforehand of achieving unsatisfying results. The other two, which have been known much longer, are education and government. [Freud, 1937c, p. 248]

Is it possible, today, to propose a definition of the *practice of psychoanalysis*? If so, what definition? Is it not somewhat presumptuous —or even utopian—to try to summarize the complex set of heterogeneous elements that go to make up psychoanalysis? Contingent on analytic technique, the practice of psychoanalysis encompasses all the potentialities of the psychoanalytic process, which itself involves an infinite range of psychic processes. It follows that any definition of psychoanalytic practice is inseparable from some representation or other of the analytic method itself.

As is clear from the above extract, as far back as 1937 Freud felt that, like education and government, psychoanalysis might well be an "impossible" profession; it seems surprising that contemporary psychoanalysts in their daily practice, a full century after the invention of the method, still have concerns about applying it correctly, testing it, and trying to improve it.

How are we to understand the fact that contemporary practitioners go on choosing this particular method for exploring the mind and addressing its disorders? What motivates psychoanalysts to devote so much energy to theoretical and clinical discussions, to confront their ideas with those of colleagues, to read so much psychoanalytic literature and to contemplate putting their own thoughts into writing? The need to escape from the loneliness that haunts the particular kind of exchange involved in the encounter with individual patients? Or—above all, perhaps—the need to communicate and to share with a like-minded community not only the implications for their own mental processes, with regard to the world in which they live, of the psychoanalytic experience, but also their thoughts about the method and the manner in which it might be transmitted?

Freud advised psychoanalysts to take an interest in art and in science; as a result, psychoanalysis has never ceased to explore new domains—from psychiatry to education, from anthropology to linguistics, from criminology to artistic creativity. Also, the psychoanalytic treatment of children and adolescents, together with the study of narcissistic and borderline states, psychosis, autism, character disorders, and psychosomatic illnesses have gradually been included in our thinking about ordinary psychoanalytic practice and the application of the method to these fields. The theoretical and technical modalities of psychoanalytic practice have developed through the constant weaving of links between new discoveries concerning individual unconscious processes and the ways in which the various social sciences consider the manifest expressions of the human mind.

Faced with the complex nature of patients' material and with the ever-widening range of analytic practice, the psychoanalyst has constantly to explore the polysemous character of the concepts that attempt to account for these. Given the paramount importance of the unconscious factor in every psychoanalytic relationship, these explorations come up against a highly specific obstacle that makes it very difficult to conceive of a meaningful representation of what psychoanalysts actually do—whether it be the analyst's own way of working or that of his or her colleagues.

In his "Analysis terminable and interminable", Freud (1937c) tried to be clear and realistic, warning his readers not only that the art of psychoanalysis is a difficult one, full of surprises and pitfalls, but also that anyone who practises that art must expect to meet with disappointment and disillusion. This leads the psychoanalyst to wonder about the strange *resistance to change* that constitutes the main obstacle to the satisfactory progress of any psychoanalytic treatment—a resistance that the analyst tries to identify by means of metaphors, the stuff that dreams are made of.

And how functional are *they* nowadays? Do analysts still think that "a lion only springs once" (Freud 1937c, p. 219)? Do they still prefer to "let sleeping dogs lie" (*ibid.*, p. 231)? In fact—and in reality—though the steep and dangerous roads leading to the "caves where the dragons of primaeval days dwell" (*ibid.*, p. 229) seem a little easier of access than before, and though psychoanalysts are somewhat more familiar with the dynamic, structural and economic cauldrons of the "Witch Metapsychology" (*ibid.*, p. 225), they still constantly come up against the same questions that assailed Freud with respect to the practice of psychoanalysis—whatever their theoretical preferences and the different means they employ to unravel the dilemmas inherent in any psychoanalytic treatment.

The best proof of this is the vast range of theoretical modalities and practical applications that run through the entire history of the psychoanalytic movement—from its vicissitudes (Ferenczi, Klein, Balint, Lacan, Winnicott, Bion, etc.) through its deviations (the history of dissident movements: Adler, Steckel, Jung, Rank, Reich, etc.) and ending with its epistemology.

Yet the question of defining the practice of analysis remains unanswered: when we speak of "practising" psychoanalysis, what exactly do we mean: what the practitioner actually does, the methodology involved, or the underlying theory on which this specific practice is based and by which it is justified?

If the question can be asked in such terms, it is immediately obvious just how interdependent practice, theory and technique are with regard to their implementation in clinical situations. It would seem, therefore, somewhat out of place to discuss the practice of psychoanalysis without some reference to its consubstantial links with those theoretical contributions which, as Freud's whole work goes to show, both support and nurture it.

Note

1. [Translator's note: The French proverb: "le mieux est l'ennemi du bien."]

CHAPTER ONE

Method and practice

The practice of psychoanalysis derives in the main from the teachings of its founder. Freud was the first to discover the universal nature of the laws that govern the workings of the unconscious, and analysis came quite rapidly to be defined, in practice, as being linked to the transference and the experience of the transference relationship. The therapeutic dimension was attributed to the application of a specifically psychoanalytic approach based on the transference relationship and its interpretation, and its sole justification was seen to be the underlying theory that both explained how it functioned and made it meaningful.

Freud, transference, and the practice of psychoanalysis

In the early days, when the psychoanalytic approach was first being developed, Freud drew up a number of guidelines and technical rules that were to become the mainstay of analytic practice. The validity of these concepts, developed over less than twenty years (1895–1915), has never since been called into question: on the analysand's side, to respect the fundamental rule (free association and reporting of dreams), and on the analyst's, the setting (the couch-and-armchair "space", regular and frequent sessions of fixed length).

Even in Freud's early papers on methodology and in his technical recommendations as to the practice of analysis, it is quite obvious that in his opinion analysis could not be based on technique alone, but also—indeed, above all—on the parameters generated by the combination, the blending, the knitting-together of clinical experience relating to the discovery of the transference—the practice of psychoanalysis by the yardstick of transference experience—*and* the theoretical elements that gave it weight.

Few of Freud's writings deal with the practical aspects of psychoanalysis as such, but it is obvious that his whole theoretical *corpus* is permeated by the very intensity of his experience as a practising analyst. In addition to the papers written between 1904 and 1918 that deal with technical matters in the strict sense of the term, the specifically clinical papers based on case reports give us some idea of how Freud worked and enable us to appreciate his activity as a clinician and practitioner of psychoanalysis.[1]

We would, however, be adopting far too narrow an approach were we to think that only those papers dealing directly with case studies can tell us something about how Freud practised analysis. All of his writings, from his metapsychological papers to those that outline his views on humanity, society, and the world in general, have something to teach us about different aspects of his work.

It is true that Freud's practice of psychoanalysis, from the outset, rested on the theoretical implications that he was eager to confirm and to illustrate; and it is also the case that every theoretical step forward, including the most speculative, was in turn constantly nourished by his practical work, which alone could confirm or refute the hypotheses he suggested. How, then, are we to define the practice of psychoanalysis?

A definition of psychoanalysis in practice

Even though Freud did not leave us a precise definition of psychoanalysis, we can all the same deduce the picture he had of it in 1923 when he suggested the following description:

> Psychoanalysis is the name (1) of a procedure for the investigation of mental processes which are almost inaccessible in any other way, (2) of a method (based upon that investigation) for the treatment of neurotic disorders and (3) of a collection of psychological information obtained along those lines, which is gradually being accumulated into a new scientific discipline. [Freud 1923a, p. 235]

We can see how, starting from this definition, psychoanalysis, in Freud's opinion, encompasses at least three different notions, each of which is related to the other two and refers back to them: *methodology*, i.e., there is a certain kind of method that lies at the heart of psychoanalysis and enables it, as distinct from other approaches, to apprehend unconscious mental processes; *therapy*, which is simply the application of that method to clinical situations; and *theory*, which takes into account the development of our knowledge of how the mind works, gradually building up (and building itself into) a theory of the mind and mental functioning.

As a result, following Freud, analysts in general would claim that the cornerstone of the practice of psychoanalysis is precisely this conjunction between clinical experience and underlying theory. Beyond this, the practice of psychoanalysis is uncompromisingly multifarious: derived from a given method, it has simultaneous clinical, technical, and theoretical dimensions.

Development of a paradigmatic model of psychoanalysis

The early days of psychoanalysis confirmed the validity of its hypotheses as to the immutable laws relating to the intrinsic existence of the unconscious and to the organization of the psychic phenomena it implies. Indeed, Freud's original followers were dedicated to verifying, illustrating, and confirming the validity of those hypotheses through their own experience.

However, once the paradigmatic model of psychoanalysis was well established, the discovery of how contradictory the transference—and hence mental life as a whole—could be quickly caused problems for an approach based solely on the first instinctual theory as defined in Freud's original topographical model, because the gap between what the theory predicted and the therapeutic results actually obtained proved to be too wide.

It is relatively easy to follow, as Freud's practice developed, the theoretical shifts that clinical experience made necessary. Broadly speaking, there were two periods: from the beginnings of psychoanalysis (1895) until the end of the First World War, and from 1920 to 1939, the year of Freud's death.

In the first period, two characteristic phases can be identified. From 1895 until approximately 1915, Freud was fine-tuning the way he practised analysis. Working within his original psychoanalytic model of the neuroses, he discovered the major role played by the transference and set about theorizing this. The neurotic model could be looked upon as a way of understanding a "pathology of memory", and as such became the cornerstone of the entire psychoanalytic method. Derived from this model, treatment focused on integrating a forgotten past that, though buried in the depths of the mind, was still very much alive. The aim of analysis was clear: to identify and elucidate the "false" transference links with respect to the analyst, thus helping to "dissolve" them. At the same time, Freud discovered the strength of the constant thrust of the instinctual drives and their sexual nature. Consequently, the importance of the object became clearer, in so far as, enmeshed in the transference net, it could be transferred on to the analyst. The work of the analysis, then, was to focus on the transference that enabled forgotten trauma, wishes, and past events to come to the fore. The psychoanalytic method, with its recommended technique, had as its fulcrum the lifting of repression and its resultant resistance. Recollection and integration in the mind of deeply-buried past events, in so far as they could be reconstructed, became the paradigmatic model for the work of psychoanalysis.

The second phase of this initial period (in 1914), was characterized by the introduction of the idea of narcissism. This concept became necessary when analysis began to come up against certain kinds of resistance to the treatment, in particular negative transference. In the same year as the concept of narcissism appeared, Freud discovered that processes involving repetition were inherent to the unfolding of the psychoanalytic process itself. As regards the transference, repetition was manifested in two ways: transference itself is repetition, and repetition unfolds through the transference. As a result, the gap almost imperceptibly widened between the kind of recollection desired by the treatment and repetition, which attempts to repeat "everything that has already made its way from the sources of the repressed into (the patient's] manifest personality—his inhibitions and unserviceable attitudes and his pathological character-traits. He also repeats all his symptoms . . ." (Freud, 1914g, p. 151).

The consequences of the "1920 turning point"

The second period (1920–1939), during which many questions were raised concerning the difficulties in and limitations to the practice of psychoanalysis (because of the widening gap between theory and practice), began with what we now call the "1920 turning point". It highlights the profound theoretical upheaval brought about by the realization of the clinical importance of the compulsion to repeat. The compulsion to repeat threw new light on the failure of certain analyses; these failed analyses demolished the established theoretical model, the paradigm being Freud's analysis of the Wolf-Man.

Given that certain types of resistance could not be overcome in analysis—I am thinking in particular of transference entropy and the resultant "negative therapeutic reaction" (Freud, 1937c, p. 243)—the model derived from the original instinctual drive and topographical theory was very quickly to prove insufficient. Though the basic concepts and the manner in which they found themselves repeated in the transference neurosis remained valid—the organization of the infantile neurosis could still be identified—they proved too vague and too restrictive when it came to recent discoveries in the practical field. The aim of analysis was still to try to overcome resistance and lift repression, but the repetitive nature of the repressed proved too powerful, so that recollection was impossible to obtain; the treatment came up against the stumbling-block of the patient's inability to confirm, via his or her own memories, the analyst's (re)constructions. The transference neurosis, in bringing past events back into the present and in reactivating the Oedipus complex, was itself an obstacle to the lifting of repression. These limits to the concept of transference neurosis and the sometimes disappointing results of analysis meant that the analytic project and the very concept of psychoanalysis itself would have to be considerably modified.

As a result, Freud postulated the existence of unconscious mental processes that have no spontaneous tendency to leave traces in the mind or be subjected to the return of the repressed. The destructive instinct, the principle obstacle to libidinal development, was henceforth added to the compulsion to repeat (with its aims that go "beyond the pleasure principle", emphasizing the "daemonic" aspect of the drive (Freud, 1920g, p. 21)). Further, the representation of intrapsychic conflict also shifted. The topographical conflict between Conscious and Unconscious gave way to an intrapsychic conflict within the ego itself. The ego, which is mainly unconscious, also nourishes the compulsion to repeat (Freud, 1923b).

Where hitherto there were only prohibition and desire, both of which could be represented in the transference neurosis, henceforth entropy, the non-representable and the impossible were to play a crucial role. Freud thereby opened the way for mental operations such as denial, splitting, disavowal, foreclosure, idealization, and projection; these contribute to the extreme forms of "the work of the negative" (Green, 1993b) and generate entropy of thinking ("anti-thinking").

For Freud, the aim of analysis remained the loosening of repression and the lifting of infantile amnesia; the main project, however, was no longer to make an inventory of the infinite contents of the unconscious but to focus on the work of transformation itself in so far as it determines the success or failure of any given analysis. Nevertheless, the practical and theoretical aspects of psychoanalysis still did not dovetail. Freud then tried to find out why in his paper on "Analysis terminable and interminable" (1937c); in this paper, he showed just how practically-minded he was, and made no secret of the fact that the difficulties and even "limits" of the psychoanalytic method and practice left him perplexed.

Freud's clinical legacy: "Analysis terminable and interminable"

In 1937, Freud was eighty-one years of age. Untiring in his researches, after more than forty years of analytic experience, he wrote "Analysis terminable and interminable" with the idea of reviewing the practice of psychoanalysis and the difficulties that analysts encounter in their work. Focusing on clinical and practical experience, this essay constitutes Freud's clinical legacy. Together with "Constructions in analysis" (1937d),[2] *Moses and Monotheism* (1939a), an illustration of how Freud conceived of applying the psychoanalytic method to other fields, and "An outline of psychoanalysis" (1940a), in which he summarizes the essential points of analytic theory, this article is part of a group of papers that make up Freud's written legacy.

Today, this essay gives us a fairly precise idea of the way in which Freud conceived of psychoanalysis through his practical experience of it. Given that we just have to accept the fact that analysis "does not always lead to the promised land" (Fain, 1987), Freud sought to investigate the various kinds of difficulty that lay in the path of every analytic treatment.

For Freud, the practice of psychoanalysis was never an end in itself. Attentive as he was to what could be learned from treating the neuroses, especially the theoretical developments, he could see that there was nevertheless a distinction between, on the one hand, the practice of analysis and its therapeutic effects, and, on the other, psychoanalytic theory and the speculations to which it may give rise. In Freud's view, if the results of an analysis do not come up to expectation, it is because certain essential concepts that would provide a theoretical explanation of the situation have not yet been developed.

In recalling certain experiences in which he had had to deal with transference phenomena marked essentially by negativity (such as his analytic adventure with the Wolf-Man, or his analytic relationship with Sandor Ferenczi, or again the one that involved one of his very first patients, Emma Eckstein), Freud tried to account for the activity and the scope of those psychic forces that set up the main obstacles to the successful course of an analysis. He had, therefore, not only to re-examine many theoretical parameters and the contradictory aspects of mental life as manifested in psychoanalysis, but also to think again about the gap between theory and practice that the analyst encounters (Donnet, 1985).

A reassessment of the practice of psychoanalysis

There are two kinds of consideration that underlie "Analysis terminable and interminable", one pertaining to practical matters, the other to theory.

The first series of reflections concerns the practice of psychoanalysis and its therapeutic effects. Freud asks several technical and practical questions: what about the idea of shortening the duration of an analysis? How long should an analysis last? What do we mean by the "end" of an analysis? Can there be such a thing as an "end" to an analysis? Is there such a thing as a natural end to an analysis? What do we mean by the term "cure"? If the patient shows improvement, what happens afterwards? Can analysis truly claim to restore "absolute psychical normality" (Freud, 1937c, pp. 219–220)? Indeed, do those words really mean anything at all? And so on.

These questions on the practice of analysis relate to the obvious gap between theory and therapeutic results; they link up with those that, in previous years, had been raised by Ferenczi's new proposals and theoretical developments. For Ferenczi, the aim of his innovations was to show that it is through practical work that theory can develop properly and prove its relevance, whereas for Freud, theory helped analysts to reflect on what they do and to explain the complex nature of the process itself, but did not necessarily resolve the practical problems raised. I shall return to this point later, for it was to be a major source of tension between Freud and Ferenczi as regards the analyst's conception of the nature and choices implied by his or her commitment to the practice of psychoanalysis; this tension, in fact, can be read between the lines of "Analysis terminable and interminable".

The second series of reflections concerns the points raised by psychoanalytic theory that alone, in Freud's eyes, could roll back the limits of analysis and reassert the ambitious nature of the analytic project. The question is that of entropy as opposed to change: certain patients are propelled into developing a negative therapeutic reaction, displaying passionate attitudes towards analysis and the analyst—sometimes long after the end of the analysis, even though the treatment itself was carried out in an apparently satisfactory manner.

In order to examine possible reasons for the absence of expected change in patients for whom a favourable outcome was initially predicted, Freud enumerates the reciprocal influences and counterbalancing movements between three decisive factors for the organization of mental life: the "influence of trauma" (Freud, 1937c,

p. 224) (the traumatic event and variability in the patient's capacity to internalize what occurs in reality—trauma is the most unpredictable of the three factors); the "constitutional strength of the instincts" (*ibid.*) (the *de jure* autonomous nature of instinctual life, the "daemonic" ego and the "dragons of primaeval days" (*ibid.*, p. 229)); and "alterations of the ego" (*ibid.*, p. 224) (as regards the nature and quality of the defence mechanisms).

The "underlying bedrock"

Freud then attempts to put into perspective certain elements of mental life that bring in their wake the kind of difficulties encountered during the course of an analysis. This leads him to examine, in the eight sections of "Analysis terminable and interminable", a certain number of factors: viz. the constitutional factor, which from the outset modifies the ability to integrate; resistance and defence mechanisms, with repression being first and foremost (though Freud points out that it is not the only mechanism at work); the compulsion to repeat; ego "alterations" (implicitly referring to splitting of the ego); "adhesiveness" and "mobility" of the libido, as opposed to its "inertia"; the negative transference and its most stubborn of manifestations, the "negative therapeutic reaction", based on a powerful feeling of unconscious guilt (Freud writes ((1937c, p. 242)) of the "need for punishment" and of the relationship between superego sadism and ego masochism); the strength of the "instinct of destruction" or "death-instinct", that opposes the action of Eros; the free-floating destructiveness that infiltrates *all* regions of the mind (i.e., the three agencies: id, ego, and superego); the link between sexuality and the destructive instincts as they emerge in the problem of homosexuality; the difficulty in tolerating the difference between the sexes (in men, homosexuality; in women, the absence of a penis); and, finally, the important question of *femininity* and the underlying biological "bedrock" (the metaphor refers to disavowal of the feminine dimension in both sexes) as the ultimate limit to any further progress in analysis.[3] Shaped by the combined action of bisexuality and the final instinctual drive theory (Eros and the death drive), the "bedrock" would thus appear to set a limit, a final frontier, to any possibility of analysis.

For Freud, it is an "underlying" bedrock:

> At no other point in one's analytic work does one suffer more from an oppressive feeling that all one's repeated efforts have been in vain, and from a suspicion that one has been "preaching to the winds", than when one is trying to persuade a woman to abandon her wish for a penis on the ground of its being unrealizable or when one is seeking to convince a man that a passive attitude to men does not always signify castration and that it is indispensable in many relationships in life. [Freud, 1937c, p. 252]

As a resistance that cannot be overcome, involving the narcissistic wound that represents in the minds of both men and women the acceptance of the feminine dimension, the "bedrock" generates, in men, a "rebellious overcompensation" and, in women, "severe depression". Freud goes on: "The repudiation of femininity can be nothing else than a biological fact, a part of the great riddle of sex" (*ibid.*).

At the point where he introduces the question of "repudiation of femininity", in the eighth and final section of his paper, Freud reminds us (*ibid.*, p. 251) that it "did not escape Ferenczi's notice"; Ferenczi had argued, some ten years before, in 1928, in an article entitled "The problem of the termination of analyses", that for an analysis to be "successful", "in females the wish for a penis and in males the struggle against passivity" have to be mastered. Though Freud was sensitive to his follower's shrewdness and acknowledged his immense talent as a clinician, he none the less writes here that, speaking from his own experience, "in this Ferenczi was asking a great deal".

For the reader who knows of the disagreement between Freud and Ferenczi that gradually deepened in the years between 1927 or 1928 and the latter's death in 1933, the posthumous reproach Freud aims at him—"in this Ferenczi was asking a great deal"—can be seen as yet another instance of Freud's growing criticism of his follower and friend; their divergence of opinion had a lot to do with the practice of analysis and, in creating a new split between theory and practice (Donnet, 1995), it heightened the already existing tension in that field.

Seen in this light, "Analysis terminable and interminable" can be read as a posthumous dialogue with Ferenczi, whose presence "haunts" Freud's paper from start to finish (Bokanowski, 1979). Freud used the dialogue to justify his own points of view and to challenge the practical aspects of his follower's innovative outlook; though Ferenczi is therein described as a "master of analysis" (Freud, 1937c, p. 230), Freud felt that he had gone too far in certain aspects of analysis and as a result had overstepped the mark of what constitutes the very specificity of Freudian doctrine.

The conflict between Freud and Ferenczi

After the turning point of 1920, Ferenczi, as ever sensitive to the clinical aspects of the compulsion to repeat but less inclined to accompany Freud along the road to the economic principle behind the destructive drive, felt that the practice of analysis and psychoanalytic therapy had still a great deal to teach us. He determined to highlight these points in a book he wrote with Otto Rank in 1924, *Entwicklungszwiele der Psychoanalyse* (*The Development of Psychoanalysis*). The aim of this book, for its authors, was to reply to a question Freud had asked in 1922 during the Berlin Congress, the theme of which was the relationship between psychoanalytic technique and theory: "To what degree does technique influence theory, to what extent are they supportive of or detrimental to each other?"

In their book, Ferenczi and Rank explore certain parameters of the then commonly-held ideas about practice. Starting with Freud's 1914 article "Remembering, repeating and working-through" (Freud ,1914g), which they discuss at some length, they suggest that it is not remembering, as Freud thought, but the compulsion to repeat—in their view, the only truly manifest expression of the transference—that should be worked on in the psychoanalytic process. They therefore recommend analysis of the experience of the transference rather than true recollection of repressed memories and fantasies: affect should be in the service of meaning. In their reassessment of the question of resistance to cure and of the limits to analysis, they refuse the idea that the castration complex is the only indication that analysis is indeed possible; for Ferenczi and Rank, the idea that narcissistic pathology represents a limitation for analysis is merely a wish to protect oneself against too deep an analysis.

Their undoubted interest in psychoanalytic technique is explored at some length, with the suggestion that an active technique (Ferenczi's term) would be more conducive to experience (*Erlebnis*) and enable the repetition of certain trauma to unfold within the psychoanalytic setting, since no other context is suitable enough for this. In discussing the mutual influence of technique on theory and vice-versa, they emphasize the circular and recursive nature of these two elements; they highlight the need to put aside all theoretical assumptions when the analytic situation is addressed: each new case should be approached afresh, that is without closing oneself to new experiences. It is obvious that Ferenczi and Rank see the material the patient brings to his or her sessions as above all implying a process that both protagonists have to work through, hence the importance of the analyst's countertransference, and that of his or her personal analysis—indeed, Ferenczi was later to insist on that as being the second fundamental rule of psychoanalysis.

Obviously, these innovative ideas, with the new horizons they opened up, could, given the times, sow the seeds of revolution. For example, to claim that the work of analysis could be envisaged from the perspective of the analyst's countertransference commitment (i.e., with respect to the *analyst's* emotions and feelings)—since it would make it easier to address the deeper levels of the mind without any *a priori* limitation imposed on regression—was a development that could be seen as a real turning point in the very conception and practice of psychoanalysis.

Two types of psychoanalytic practice

Accordingly, Ferenczi refused to attribute to the patient sole responsibility for any negative trends ("negative therapeutic reactions") or contradictions that emerge in the transference; he suggested that difficulties arising in the course of an analysis are due at least in part to blind spots in the analyst's countertransference. In the years that followed, he discussed the theory-vs-practice issue more in terms of the fact that there were two analytic modalities and two types of analytic practice: Freud's "classic" pattern on the one hand, and Ferenczi's own, less "orthodox" and more in-depth model on the other. The former, based essentially on the paternal aspect of the transference, on the undoing of repression, on recollection and reconstruction, leads, via the encounter between representation and transference, to interpretation and working-through, the "aim" and "end" of analysis, together with insight (*Einsicht*). Ferenczi's model focuses more on the primary aspects of relationships and the maternal transference, and it introduces both the concept of object relations and the role these play as the treatment progresses; this is a "regressive" analysis, the main aspects of which are experiential, interactive, infra-verbal and empathic (*Einfühlung*). It enables the analyst to make direct contact with the child in the patient (the patient's infantile dimension) and thereby to discover the trauma to which the patient had been subjected.[4]

Ferenczi thus found himself facing complex transference situations with very difficult patients whom no other analyst would take on, as his colleagues readily acknowledged. He invented new technical guidelines and hypotheses that led him little by little to reassess and modify the setting in a way that today would be called testing it out (Cahn, 1983). Forced to abandon his "active" technique because it sometimes ended in failure, Ferenczi pleaded for greater "elasticity" in technique ("relaxation" or "neocatharsis") with the aim of addressing and treating clinical situations of a highly impassioned nature. In interpreting the transference these generated as a mere repetition (the compulsion to repeat) of childhood trauma, Ferenczi had to re-examine and reflect on the concept of trauma itself. He widened the question of seduction beyond Freud's hypotheses and gave the concept fresh impetus by considering the etiological impact of trauma as the result either of a "mental rape" of the child by an adult, or of a "confusion of tongues" between them, or again of the adult's denial of the child's "despair". From this point of view, the clinical situations of the patients in whom Ferenczi was interested were characterized not so much by the natural destiny of their libido as by extreme states of mental (and sometimes physical) distress leading to the death throes of mental life.

Ferenczi reflected a great deal on these developments between 1928 and 1933, and they inevitably drew him into conflict with Freud. A theoretical gulf—quite literally—opened up between them, with the concept of infantile trauma forming the fault line. For Freud, considering the compulsion to repeat as a repetition of a traumatic situation and holding the object responsible for this was tantamount to underestimating the resources of the mind and its ability to transform both trauma and the mental pain that attaches to it (Green, 1990). In his scepticism, Freud saw in Ferenczi's innovations a regression—and indeed a theoretical deviation—with the inherent risk of going back to the ideas he had himself abandoned after his 1897 "neurotica".

The "unanalysed negative transference"

"Analysis terminable and interminable" is Freud's attempt to explain the limitations he saw to thinking about practical issues and the exercise of psychoanalysis. In the background, however, the paper also tries to understand—posthumously—the reasons that led Ferenczi to go beyond the then frontiers of psychoanalysis; these speculations are expressed in latent fashion in the passage where Freud discusses the reproaches Ferenczi formulated concerning his "unanalysed negative transference". I explore this issue in more detail in Chapter Six, where I discuss the refusal of the feminine dimension and negative tendencies.

If we read between the lines of Freud's 1937 paper, we can identify the questions he was asking himself: how could a man like Ferenczi, who was a "master of analysis", not recognize that therapy is only one application among others of psychoanalytic theory? How could he have breached the frontiers of analysis and refuse its theoretical and technical limitations? How could he have wanted, by rushing headlong into therapeutic activity, to return at all costs to the practical experience of therapy and create at the same time new techniques that called into question the established setting? How could he have taken the resultant risk of drawing the practice of analysis into such a transgressive perspective?

We know that, for a long time, the paralysing impact of this divergence of opinion meant that it was impossible for the psychoanalytic community to become involved in the argument between the Master and his brilliant disciple; it took another two, or even three, generations of analysts before sufficient progress could be made for Ferenczi's ideas to be recognized as the source of developments that would be recommended for treating states of mind that we call today the "extended" indications of psychoanalysis ("difficult" cases, "borderline", and "non-neurotic" personalities, etc.). Their central emphasis is on the wish to apprehend and to identify certain crucial factors at the heart of the psychoanalytic process, and as a result they have encouraged the idea that other parameters may be used in order to make an analysis intelligible. In turn, these new parameters have opened up fresh theoretical and practical horizons (Bokanowski, 1997). Ferenczi's ideas meant also that it became possible to conceive of a much wider range of indications for psychoanalytic treatment—in particular those that come under the heading of "narcissistic" pathology, the result of some deficiency in mental categories that depend on "primary" aspects (reaching towards primary repression, going beyond representation in order to make contact with the "narcissistic splitting" that lies behind repression). Last, they made for new modalities in the way analysts listen to and understand their patients (working on the psychoanalyst's countertransference as well as on the perception of what the patient is expressing); this in turn led to a fundamental change in the way we look on the analyst's role, the countertransference and the psychoanalytic setting, and made regression more meaningful in that it became possible to go beyond the theoretical model of reconstruction.[5]

Beyond the misunderstanding between Freud and Ferenczi, related as it was to their psychoanalytic and intersubjective history, the interesting questions that the controversy raised essentially involved the kinds of tension that emerge, with respect to the method of psychoanalysis and its applications, every time psychoanalytic thinking is faced with the epistemological leaps that inevitably crop up from time to time as it develops.

From one controversy to another

The situation between Freud and Ferenczi cannot fail to bring to mind another controversy that was to take place some ten years later between Anna Freud and Melanie Klein—and here again the issues involved related to the practice of psychoanalysis and the manner in which it is influenced by theory. Klein's theoretical and technical developments brought her into conflict with those who, behind Anna Freud, reproached her for deviating from orthodox Freudian theory; time and time again Klein had to defend the idea that if we were to reject the hypotheses generated by clinical practice on the ground that they appeared to contradict established theory, we would dry up the fountain of progress at its source. She was convinced that it was not the letter but the spirit of Freud's discoveries that should be followed, and felt that experience of the analytic method should take pride of place over established theory (King & Steiner, 1992).

These historical examples show how every analyst, confronted with a hiatus between theory and practice, is bound to ask questions about the practice of analysis in general and about his or her experience in particular: "Given this gap between theory and practice, to what extent does my way of doing things correspond to theory and feel the stronger for it?", or, conversely, "Given this gap between theory and practice, to what extent can my way of doing things be carried out without any reference to theory?"

Faced with such questions and with the impact they have on the practice of psychoanalysis, every analyst inevitably feels the need to leave the isolation of his or her consulting-room and seek support in working out these difficulties through clinical and theoretical discussions with other colleagues. Based on personal experience, and whatever the theoretical parameters they consciously think they adopt, such discussions help analysts to follow more or less in the footsteps of Freud when he had to make an epistemological break with the past (in going from the first to the second topographical theory); at the same time, we can learn more about the various epistemological breaks that occurred when his followers went on developing his ideas (Klein, Balint, Winnicott, Lacan, Bion, Kohut, etc.). If we as analysts can refrain from trying to fill the gap between theory and practice with *a priori* ideas, we will be able to remain open to the vicissitudes of the infinite set of processes in the human mind and have the good fortune to feel emerging from within ourselves some truly creative images.

Notes

1. See *Studies on Hysteria* (1895d), "Fragment of an analysis of a case of hysteria" (1905e), "Notes upon a case of obsessional neurosis" (1909d),

"From the history of an infantile neurosis" (1918b), and "The psychogenesis of a case of female homosexuality" (1920a).

2. "Constructions in analysis" can be looked upon as complementary to "Analysis terminable and interminable". However, since I am more concerned here with the theoretical modalities of intervention and interpretation in their attempts to assist reconstruction, I shall no longer refer to the former paper in the rest of this chapter. Hence, when I mention in the following pages "the 1937 paper", I am referring to "Analysis terminable and interminable".
3. The reader will have noticed that Freud's 1937 paper clearly shows the supremacy of psychic factors linked to the development of the second structural theory; this is all the more striking in that Freud has nothing to say about certain other important factors related to his invention of the original topographical theory (for example, the problems involved in mourning or in narcissism).
4. At that time too, Melanie Klein was laying the foundations of her own theory and constructing a certain number of hypotheses about what, in her view, governed the organization of the early Oedipus complex.
5. As is well known, relationships between, on the one hand, primary and primal dimensions and, on the other, the traditional Oedipal ones, lie at the heart of the clinical and practical issues I am discussing in this chapter.

CHAPTER TWO

Concepts in contemporary psychoanalytic practice

There is at present a considerable number of techniques that claim to be able to cure mental suffering and even pride themselves on that fact—hypnosis, Gestalt therapy, Dasein therapy, transactional analysis, micro-psychoanalysis, primal scream, re-birthing, non-analytic relaxation, cognitive and behavioural psychotherapies, etc., to name but a few.

On what grounds can we argue that there exists a crucial difference between psychoanalysis as we know it and these other techniques that all claim to be psychotherapeutic? Unlike any of these, psychoanalysis is the only psychotherapeutic method that, after recognizing the fundamental significance of the Unconscious in the organization of the human mind, invented a specific technique for investigating that Unconscious and its manifest expressions with the help of the conscious and interactive part of the individual. The technique is based on the tendency to repeat inherent in all mental processes, as well as on an essential feature of the instinctual drives: the opportunity to displace cathexes on to new objects.

The practice of psychoanalysis, therefore, is inconceivable without the idea of repetition, in the transference, of past cathexes; it requires also the ability to use and to analyse the transference. The aim of psychoanalytic treatment is to identify and develop the creative powers of the Unconscious and its virtually inexhaustible modes of expression. There can be no question, therefore, of using a technique the only aim of which is to do away with symptoms, modify behaviour, or adjust to the environment—far less to strive after tangible goals or visible success. Psychoanalysis is for those who feel some curiosity about how their mental life develops and who accept the risk of having to bear the inevitable distress that such an investigation entails.

Though it does, as a result, address a very specific domain, there is no doubt that the practice of psychoanalysis is none the less heterogeneous, given the many and varied contributions all psychoanalysts make to the common wealth of experience. Individual experiences bear witness to the infinite variety of forms of expression in the Unconscious, and the heterogeneous nature of psychoanalysis can be felt in both the field of theory and in that of its applications.

Heterogeneity in psychoanalytic practice: one approach or several?

As I pointed out in the previous chapter, Freud's entire *œuvre* and the developments his followers gave to it make it clear that, given the difficulties involved in the practice of analysis, psychoanalytic theory and practice have never stopped evolving, and this from their very inception.

In the analysis of apparently neurotic patients, the emergence of psychotic nuclei, perverse defences, unexpected regression, character defences, narcissistic troubles and passionate transference (transference hatred and persistent negative therapeutic reactions) soon led psychoanalysts to admit that the theoretical model of the neuroses, though still absolutely necessary, could no longer be thought of as the unified general model of psychoanalytic theory, given its inadequacies as regards these pathological conditions.

When analysts had to confront the difficulty of finding an appropriate method for treating these disturbances and for making a detailed study of them on the conceptual level, many of them—mainly in the wake of the developments carried out by the Kleinians and post-Kleinians between 1930 and 1960—decided to focus on how best to approach these "difficult" cases. Accordingly, there took place both an extension of the indications for psychoanalysis and a development of the theoretical models that attempted to account for the difficulties that emerged in the course of certain treatments and in the experience of the analytic partnership.

To the original model of psychoanalysis—the classic model that linked defence psychoneuroses, transference neurosis and infantile neurosis—were progressively added the object relations model and an interest in the manner in which the mental functioning of analyst and patient connected together. These models, which extended and considerably enriched those that Freud left us, enabled the conception of psychoanalytic practice to break fresh ground. The focus on resistance (removal of obstacles and insight) was gradually replaced by interest in the psychoanalytic process with respect to the patient's mental functioning, then by attention to the object of the work being undertaken by both patient and analyst (the analytic space), via the study of their *hic et nunc* communication in the actual session. In turn, these developments brought contemporary psychoanalysts back to the parameters that govern the workings of the human mind, issues that had preoccupied Freud as early as 1895 ("A project for a scientific psychology") and again in 1911 (Freud, 1911b).[1]

It is therefore impossible nowadays to discuss the practice of psychoanalysis without making some reference to the various currents of thought that, since Freud's day, have accompanied the evolution of that practice. More than sixty years ago now, Fairbairn wondered whether the libido was pleasure-seeking or object-seeking; that question laid the foundations for a whole series of conceptions and models of the way the mind works. There are those that involve the vagaries of the relationship with the internal object or of object relations as a whole; different analysts have approached these issues in quite distinct ways (such as, for example, Klein, Balint, Spitz, and Maurice Bouvet). At the same time, interest in the psychoanalytic process as such has gradually increased, and now covers many fields:

- the organization, within the analysis itself, of the inner workings of the patient's mind;

- the focus of the work carried out by patient and analyst in terms of the communication that takes place between them and/or as a result of that communication. Hence such notions as "the analytical situation" (Baranger), "the space of the analysis" (Viderman), the "thirdness" that is implied by the space between analyst and analysand (Green)—as well as, from quite another standpoint, those theoretical currents that led to emphasis being placed on "the intersubjective relationship";
- the links between the manner in which the analyst's mind works and the way he or she "functions" with that particular patient (Winnicott);
- the direct links with the patient's mental functioning (Bion);
- the importance of the analytical setting (Bleger, J.-L. Donnet, Green, etc.) and of its facilitating ability (Winnicott's "facilitating environment");
- working at and with the "frontiers", the term being understood both as a concept in its own right and as what Green has called "areas of mental processing".

Because of the different points of view to which these dimensions give rise, their conceptual developments make it clear that the many and varied parameters involved have had to be identified and explored as they apply to the practice of psychoanalysis. These parameters organize the mental processes that are at work within the analysis—sometimes, indeed, they hinder its more or less smooth progress and development (the ideal model of which is still the paradigmatic analytical treatment).

In parallel to this extension of the practical domain, another problem emerged—that of gathering together theoretical and technical criteria and trying to make them homogenous. Though the basic tenets are shared by all practitioners,[2] points of divergence do emerge from time to time between the various schools of thought; such disagreements are often brought about by new discoveries in clinical practice. Consequently, the use analysts make of the theoretical *corpus*, as regards clinical and practical matters, must vary to some extent at least. As the reader will see below, it depends also, in the main, on the complex subjective relationship analysts have with Freud's theoretical *corpus*.

To illustrate this point, we need look no further than what Laplanche and Pontalis have to say in *The Language of Psychoanalysis* apropos of their definition of transference: "The reason it is so difficult to propose a definition of transference is that for many authors the notion has taken on a very broad extension (. . .). As a result, the concept is burdened down more than any other with *each* analyst's particular views on the treatment—on its objective, dynamics, tactics, scope, etc." (Laplanche & Pontalis, 1967 (1973, p. 456, italics added).

There is obvious disagreement among analysts of different schools of thought; but we can observe just as often that there are also differences of opinion among analysts who belong to the same school of thought and who are in frequent communication with one another. This is proof, if proof were needed, of the vitality of the Freudian *corpus*. Freud himself never stated or claimed that his theory should remain untouched; on the contrary, in all of his writings, he demonstrated that it was in the very nature of psychoanalysis to be capable of thinking through new theoretical developments and of integrating them with earlier discoveries.

Concepts and practice

From the point of view of psychoanalytic theory, a settled conceptual basis does exist and is generally accepted, at least consciously. This foundation upon which the Freudian *corpus* is built and from which it takes its strength comprises the following four "fundamental" concepts: the unconscious, the constant pressure of the instinctual drives, the existence of sexuality in children, and repression.[3]

These cornerstone concepts, together with the many others that have taken these as their basis and have gone on to develop as psychoanalysis itself progressed more and more, have been considerably worked over and enriched by successive generations of analysts, from Freud to the present day. This is particularly the case—though the list is far from complete—of narcissism, object relations, affect, identification, anxiety, regression, symbol-formation, remembering and reconstruction, trauma, seduction, primal fantasies, the structure of ego, superego, and id, psychic reality, negation, denial, splitting, masochism, the death drive, etc. . . .[4]

Depending on the period and the theoretical sensitivity prevalent in different analytic groups, these concepts and their developments have had varying degrees of success. Many have had an immediate and enriching impact on the analytic *corpus*, but some others have not been fully accepted, reassessed, and integrated within the general framework of Freudian metapsychology; among the latter, there have even been instances of new concepts losing their theoretical density and as a result having a somewhat reductive influence on psychoanalytic thinking as a whole.

The paramount illustration of this situation is Freud's hypothesis of the death drive. As is well known, that hypothesis gave rise to impassioned debates within the psychoanalytic community, both during Freud's lifetime and afterwards. For Winnicott, for example, the death instinct was a concept that Freud introduced because he had no inkling whatsoever of the primitive love impulse (Winnicott, 1952, quoted in Winnicott, 1987, and also: "I simply cannot find value in (Freud's) idea of a Death Instinct", Winnicott, 1962[1965], p. 177)

In France, ten years or so ago, this hypothesis (which Freud himself felt to be of the utmost significance) was debated at some length. Though the psychoanalysts involved all concurred in accepting the same well-established concepts, three currents of thought, three divergent tendencies, none the less emerged (Bokanowski, 1989):

- the concept of the death drive has no practical use and should therefore be abandoned in both theory and practice. These analysts felt that the concept was unclear and could not be taken as axiomatic (Bergeret, 1987), or that it was unnecessarily de-sexualizing. Recourse was had to it only when complications in working through difficulties pertaining to some missing element or dimension (Guillaumin, 1987) were encountered. For those who opposed the concept for reasons of theory, the death drive was one of the prevalent myths of psychoanalysis.
- the death instinct is a genuinely antagonistic and complementary drive, mixed in varying proportions with Eros. For those who support this point of view, the work of the Eros–Thanatos pairing is crucial and, as a result, representative of the "life instinct" (Le Guen, 1989).

- the death drive is a fundamental principle that can account for the negativity lying at the heart of every instinctual drive. For these analysts, the death drive is central to the work of the negative dimension that leads to defusion, disruption, destruction, fragmentation, dislocation, de-cathexis and de-objectalization (Green, 1986b).

This example tends to show that the (pre-)conceptions of analytic treatment and the technical (pre-)suppositions of these analysts will differ, depending on which of the three theoretical positions they adopt. This would seem to be the case in particular as regards the importance and role they attribute to their counter-transference involving patients who confront them with clinical borderline situations that are close to the outer frontiers of analysability. In such circumstances, where the analyst's counter-transference is put severely to the test, the de-objectalizing function of the instinctual drives is particularly acute.

The presence of theory in the mind of the analyst

Since clinical experience cannot claim to speak for itself independently of any theoretical option, it is easy to imagine that an analyst's theoretical concerns will weigh heavily on his or her technical and practical decisions. This raises the question of the presence and significance of theory—in other words, of metapsychology—in the analyst's thinking. Narcissistic cathexis of theory is often directly related to a narcissistic wound concerning the daily obligation to work with the unconscious against repression; but it is none the less crucial, during the time devoted to the practice of consultation and analysis, that the psychoanalyst manages to put aside his or her theorizing activity in order to give free rein to focusing on what is being expressed in the session. The possibility remains that, with this kind of emotional communication, theoretical (re)discovery can only be made as an "after"-thought.

This is the price to pay if we are to avoid the reductive dilemma that consists in wondering whether theory—and, implicitly, the interpretation the analyst has of it—makes what patients say meaningful or whether meaning is already contained in what they express, already present and historically constituted in their Unconscious. That important question was for a long time at the heart of psychoanalysis and analytic practice: it connects with the question that was at one point felt to be crucial to the theoretical debate concerning remembering and reconstruction:[5] is the patient's so-called recollection of childhood events in fact a reconstruction? If so, what are the consequences for the psychoanalytic process? That crucial debate, opposing those for whom construction should lead to the objective reality of the patient's past and those for whom reality can only be known and recognized through the interpretation the mind has of it (or has suggested to it), did not always take into account a third possible approach that could contribute an additional dimension to the problem of recollection/reconstruction: putting into words the state of the patient's unconscious relationship with the analyst, thereby offering a new dimension to the history (or historicity) of the internal object or objects that the analyst at that point represents for the patient.

The polysemous nature of the theoretical references psychoanalysts have in mind both enhances their practical work and makes it much more complex. None the less, the particularities of the unconscious interaction between practice and theory to which analysts are constantly referred enable them not only to avoid reifying theory but also to tolerate the idea that any definitive theoretical truth can at best be uncertain—and that is all to the benefit of the development of their own reflective and integrative abilities.

The specific nature of psychoanalytic practice

The conceptual treasures produced by the proliferation of theoretical ideas and by the diversity—some would say the "Babelization"—of psychoanalytic thinking multiply the number of analytic dialects and force all analysts to become polyglot. In such a situation, analysts have naturally enough to create, following the thread of their practical activity, their own individual and specific conception of what they do. This will reflect the personal mental pattern and subjective choices that led them to opt implicitly for one set of theoretical references rather than another; the way they practise psychoanalysis bears witness to their analytic style and to their ability to see and understand theoretical issues from an analytic perspective.

In accordance with their experience of the practice of analysis and the need to take into account the many and varied conflicting (and sometimes contradictory) theories—proof that Freudian doctrine has not stood still—psychoanalysts find themselves creating a theoretical patchwork; this may lead to attempts to relate, for example, the Freudian concept of "instinctual drive" with Lacan's "signifier", Klein's "good" or "bad" breast, Winnicott's "paradox" (the relationship between the subjective object and the object perceived objectively, or even the found/created object) (Winnicott, 1967), Bion's "alpha-function" and Green's "structuring framework" (negative hallucination), etc.

Such "tinkering" with theory is gradually built up over the long years an analyst devotes to training; it is continually put to the test not only by whatever occurs in the course of his or her psychoanalytic practice but also during (and after) the time allotted for communication and discussion: supervision, seminars, clinical and theoretical debates, meetings, scientific conventions, reading, projects for articles, etc. This can help the analyst to avoid falling into the clutch of certain dogmatic views—and hence to avoid becoming a "preacher", committed to a "cause", brandishing a banner whose colours have more to do with religion or politics than with psychoanalysis.

It will then be easier to accept the uncertain nature of theory and to venture into the "unknown": to allow the unknown within oneself to operate, to let oneself be interrogated by the relationship with the unknown (Rosolato, 1978) in order to give the unconscious a chance to discover what it is capable of revealing. In analysis, it is when we go towards our own selves that we are more able to meet what is foreign to us (David, 1984).

Resistance to infantile aspects

Every psychoanalyst's relationship with theory is in fact a relationship with his or her *own* theory, caught up in personal history and the analytic past, constituted by his or her personal analysis, psychoanalytic training and discussions within the relevant

Institute. The network of meaning constructed during one's own analysis derives from the different dialectical moments of infantile conflict projected on to the analyst and the analytic setting and processed in the transference. The daily work with patients, with the self-analytic phase this requires, further develops this network.

Just as the relationship between analyst and theory is brought into one's personal analysis, so it is drawn into the theory that gave it foundation and structure. This implies that the theoretical model of every analyst is just as dependent on his or her infantile sexual theories as on the Freudian theory that forms the basis for interpreting the activity of the Unconscious. As Donnet points out (1985), an analyst's theory is in intimate contact with its obverse: the unconscious fantasy of its creator. In other words, the analyst's theoretical apparatus operates continually on two levels: the unconscious theoretical level derived from his or her own unconscious infantile sexual theories, and a more conscious theoretical level acquired in the course of personal analysis.

An analyst's theoretical apparatus is always open to challenge by the countertransference work to which patients subject it; as a result, the analyst is able to continue analysing his or her own unconscious drive impulses and their repression. This in turn implies that, as analysts, we quite naturally call into question the theory we have constructed and go on working on it. This task further develops each time we read Freud's writings, as well as through contacts with our fellow analysts. Our identity as analysts is based on a complex mode of relationship between, on the one hand, the "child of the instinctual drives" we each of us have within us, and, on the other, the different variations of our infantile sexual theories, in the way that Freudian doctrine construes them.

Indeed, our taste for theory can be attributed to the association between our infantile sexual theories and Freudian doctrine. However, given their object—the Unconscious—our psychoanalytic theories cannot avoid our own blind spots, which constitute factors of resistance as regards the "child of the instinctual drives" and the Infantile dimension constantly at work within us (Guignard, 1996). By extension, we could suggest that every theory—and the use an analyst makes of it—contains the seeds of the blind spots that produce resistance to the Infantile dimension. From that point of view, the psychoanalytic theory that we analysts create or adopt as our own (our theoretical apparatus) has a somewhat paradoxical status: caught up in some of our blind spots relating to infantile impulses, it is none the less supportive in that it enables us to overcome resistance to other aspects of these.

The need to make contact with the Other's unconscious inevitably arouses unconscious anxiety and guilt in every analyst with respect to the sexual and incestuous fantasy aspects implied in the analytic situation. Given these circumstances, it is imperative that we create possibilities for disengagement and sublimation by means of our epistemophilic drives. In this sense, when an analyst has recourse to analytic theory, this does not in itself imply resistance or reaction formation. On the contrary, theory offers us the opportunity of organizing a setting that can enable us to contain the situation and, thereby, to protect the analytic partnership. In this case, theory operates as a frame of reference for the psychoanalyst—both an internal framework as a protective shield against stimuli (with respect to our own narcissistic or object-related infantile drive impulses) *and* an external one that, like a compass, offers direction and guidelines. It can happen, of course, that instead of functioning in an associative manner in a given session we resort in an inappropriate way to theory—*this* indeed would imply resistance with respect to the necessary topographical regression that alone can enable our primary processes and affects to circulate freely.

The referential role of theory

Resistance to the Infantile dimension could be expressed as a certain type of practice of analysis in which the support of theory is centred exclusively on one or the other of the structural conceptions, with no reference being made to the other—the first topographical theory is dismissed outright in favour of the second, or vice-versa. As I argued in the previous chapter, we know, thanks to Ferenczi, that the idea of two types of mutually-exclusive clinical approach—the one organized around castration anxiety and the Oedipus complex, the other involving narcissism, pregenital aspects and regression—can no longer hold water. The experience of psychoanalytic work puts us in touch with states of mind in which conflict organization is based, in the one individual, on the many different levels at which mental functioning is activated.

Mainly, however, it is the sometimes unconscious wish to extricate theory from its infantile roots that can constitute, for an analyst, one of the most pernicious of resistances against analytic theory and practice. I have only to mention the fate of certain metaphoric expressions employed by some of the most productive of our fellow analysts in their attempt to explain certain major theoretical and clinical developments. Lacan's "Name-of-the-father" and "foreclosure", Winnicott's "good-enough mother", Stein's "imaginary child", Braunschweig and Fain's "censorship of the (female) lover", Green's "dead mother", Anzieu's "skin-ego"—these metaphors, and others like them, had great success in the eyes of the general public interested in psychoanalysis (and of psychoanalysts themselves), given their meaningful impact on clinical practice and on metapsychology. However, if as analysts we do not systematically relate these ideas *inter alia* to the theory of the duality of instinctual drives—and do we always do this?—they may contribute to evacuating the "referential" or "landmark" role of theoretical thinking; the danger then is that they promote thinking processes based essentially on connotation, a procedure that can only reinforce resistance to our Infantile dimension.[6]

Notes

1. Other writers who have developed fresh ideas in this field include Winnicott, Bion and, more recently, Green.
2. See the *Revue Française de Psychanalyse*, *52*(5), 1988.
3. It is of some interest to note that Lacan, in his 1964 *Seminar* on *The Four Fundamental Concepts of Psychoanalysis* emphasizes the following: unconscious, instinctual drives, transference, and repetition. See Lacan (1964).
4. Other concepts, derived from new theoretical proposals that enable fresh light to be thrown on certain contradictions encountered in clinical work, have gradually been added to this traditional list. I would give special mention to the concepts of pathological (Klein) and normal (Bion) projective identification, the paradox of the found/created object (Winnicott, 1963, 1967), negative hallucination as a framework structure (Green), etc.

5. That debate was very much to the fore in France some thirty years ago. See in particular Pasche (1974) and Viderman (1974).
6. This idea was originally suggested to me by Claude Janin. See Bokanowski & Janin (1994).

CHAPTER THREE

The work of psychoanalysis

Even though the practice of analysis, as it presents itself to our thinking, with its objects and its elements, is rich in contrasts and contradictions—apparently, at any rate—we cannot completely ignore the demands imposed by our concern for consistency in practice and for coherence in psychoanalytic theory. We have no choice but to admit that, in so far as the practice of analysis can be identified as such, a common set of values precedes any explicitly individual value system. It is necessary, therefore, for analysts to be able to share some representation of the psychoanalytic process and its theoretical and practical implications. In spite of its diversity—some would say over and beyond its diversity—the work of psychoanalysis is organized and developed around a certain number of parameters that define its specificity.

The analytic space

The analytic space is the locus par excellence, saturated in affect, that allows the transference to unfold and the transference neurosis to develop and be analysed. Thus, an essential feature of the analytic space is that the dynamics of the process that develops therein are structured around the encounter between two imaginary dimensions that, in each participant, set up resistances: in the patient, the unfolding of the transference and the development of the transference neurosis, in the analyst, via the countertransference. The affects aroused by the transference neurosis and those involved in the analyst's countertransference, though different in structure, dynamics, and intensity, contribute to the organization of the analytic space, the domain that makes possible the development of the psychoanalytic process.

The many contemporary authors who have focused particularly on the analytic space and its relationship to the way the mind functions would seem to hold similar views on the concept and what it implies. Bion, for whom the relationship between mental space and analytic space is similar to that between explored space and astronomical space, wrote: "mental space (is) a thing-in-itself that is unknowable, but that can be represented by thoughts" (Bion, 1970, p. 11). Viderman puts it another way: analytic space is imaginary and ambiguous; structured by the transference and countertransference, it enables the psychoanalytic process to develop thanks both to the distortions revealed within it and to the resistances, without which no truth could ever be discovered in the process that unfolds therein (Viderman, 1977).

To the extent that the psychoanalytic space is supported by the setting, the development of the process that occurs therein becomes meaningful thanks to the analyst's work of interpretation. As Bleger points out, the analytic setting is a silent, soundless backdrop, a constant factor that enables the variables in the process to be brought into play (Bleger, 1967). It is a "not-me" that only reveals its existence by default; as an organizing element, its function is to contain, and it operates independently of the wishes of the two protagonists in the analytic situation. With respect to the psychoanalytic process, the setting serves as a neutral element; in this sense, it is a protective shield allowing for topographical regression, a kind of compass for the vertex that is being explored within the analytic space.

Interpretation is the indispensable complement of the setting; it is the all-important instrument, the true cornerstone that in itself enables work to be done on the analysand's psyche. Interpretation operates in different modes, from verbal comment to reconstruction via transference interpretations (interpretation of the transference and in the transference), and it enables links to be made between two or more latent elements that until then had remained unconscious. As a reflection of the inter- and intra-psychic processes that are taking place, the work of interpretation, like the working-through (*Durcharbeitung*) that is its consequence, enables the unconscious psychic representations (unconscious fantasy) that breathe life into what is being played out on the analytic stage to be revealed and identified with some degree of precision.

Psychoanalysis: two people working together at "transformation"

Psychoanalysis as a therapeutic undertaking implies two people working together at transformation. Set up in the analytic situation by the encounter between them and by the developing operations of two minds, the work unfolds in infinite loops in a manner that is simultaneously synchronic and diachronic. Thanks to the twin movements of identification and counter-identification between analyst and analysand, to the ceaseless attempt to correct and reformulate interpretative hypotheses and to the processes of working-through and analytic elucidation this implies, the work of psychoanalysis enables certain kinds of transformation to take place, though ultimate fulfilment always remains asymptotic. What we can expect from these changes is that they allow the patient to be more creative in his or her mind, that they reduce the effects of the compulsion to repeat and that they give new meaning to past history by enabling it to be transformed into memories. The work of analysis is organized around the following four cardinal points: transference neurosis (or psycho-neurosis), resistance, counter-transference, and interpretation.

Transference neurosis (psycho-neurosis)

As Freud argued, when we speak of transference we really mean to employ the term in its plural form, usually characterized either by their positive or negative valence or by the objects to which they refer (father, mother, brother, sister, etc.) or again by the psychic impulse that lies behind them (tenderness, passion, eroticism, aggressiveness, hatred, persecution, idealization, narcissism, ambivalence, guilt, etc.). To the question "What are transferences?", Freud replied:

> They are new editions or facsimiles of the tendencies and phantasies which are aroused and made conscious during the progress of the analysis; but they have this particularity, which is characteristic for their species, that they replace some earlier person by the person of the physician. [Freud, 1905e, p. 116]

None the less, though we accept that transferences are never univocal, we tend for the sake of convenience to use the term in the singular.

Transference is a necessary tool in every psychoanalytic treatment, where it is both an obstacle to analysis and its essential instrument. In this sense, it is, as Freud wrote to Pfister (Freud 1963a), a cross that has to be borne, yet, at the same time, as regards the work of the analysis, a blessing, since its very existence enables us to discover and to understand the patient's unconscious fantasies, those that in his or her childhood became organized around repressed emotional links; thanks to the analysis, these links are displaced (transferred) on to the analyst and are reactivated within the analytic relationship. As Freud put it: "Transference, which seems ordained to be the greatest obstacle to psycho-analysis, becomes its most powerful ally, if its presence can be detected each time and explained to the patient" (*ibid.*, p. 117).

In the analytic situation, the transference unfolds and is expressed via the transference neurosis, an artificial illness generated by the analysis. This artificial neurosis, a condensation of the whole clinical neurosis, focuses on the relationship between analysand and analyst: "The new condition has taken over all the features of the illness; but it represents an artificial illness which is at every point accessible to our intervention" (Freud, 1914g, p. 154). The analyst waits and hopes for the transference neurosis precisely because it is the motive force behind every analysis. A new edition of the clinical neurosis, it is constituted by and around the elucidation of that illness. It reactivates the memory traces linked to the development of infantile sexuality (activation or reactivation, in the present, of the analysand's past, revival of the Oedipus complex), and it makes the patient re-experience original wounds, loss of love, and painful feelings from the past associated with distress, scars, and loss of self-esteem. Like the transferences that structure and motivate it, the transference neurosis is the source both of progress and of resistance. For example, confronted with the lifting of infantile amnesia, the ego tries to maintain its coherence through the operation of repression, which reinforces splitting within the ego or between the ego and those drives it cannot or will not acknowledge; repetitive sameness is an obstacle to change. Without the transference neurosis and without the processes that lead to its unfolding through the many guises it can adopt (tender, erotic, aggressive, guilty, ambivalent, hateful, etc.) with respect to significant objects of childhood, interpretation would have no foundation on which to base its hypotheses.

Resistance

Resistances to analysis are an integral part of the psychoanalytic process and map out the characteristic features of the space that structures it. The analysis of the patient's resistances relating to highly charged and eloquent transference reactions (given their repetitive character in the analysand's past), together with the analysis of the defensive operations (countertransference) stimulated by the transference neurosis are, as far as the analyst is concerned, a constant feature of the work of any analysis. In other words, the impact of the patient's resistances and of the analyst's "counter"-resistance organizes the psychoanalytic process in relation to each participant's affects.

It is obvious that every psychoanalyst functions with a set of resistances that are relatively moderate or at least can be made so; a necessary evil, they are also a necessary good. To consider the analyst's resistances in a way similar to the manner in which countertransference was regarded in the early days of psychoanalysis—as an obstacle rather than as an indispensable instrument for making progress in the analytic work—would nowadays be seen as misconstruing, or even failing completely to understand, what the psychoanalytic process is all about.

Given that resistance to the Unconscious is unlimited—this indeed is one of the properties of resistance—how could any analyst ever imagine having finished once and for all with his or her own resistances to psychoanalysis? How could any analyst even think of claiming that he or she has indeed done so? If we cannot reconcile ourselves to the fact that no one ever manages to get to the bottom of these resistances, that in itself would mean that remnants of our infantile omnipotence, with its megalomaniac and perhaps paranoid aims, are still active, the ultimate degree of resistance to psychoanalysis. Having to reconcile ourselves to never seeing the end of our resistances is even more painful for our narcissism in that, because of the constant pressure of the instinctual drives, the task is a never-ending one.

We analysts have sometimes to consider what determines the future outcome of our resistances, preventing us in the course of an analysis from feeling ourselves to be (or to be experienced any longer as) a "potential analyst" (Enriquez, 1977) for a given patient. This leads to the question—always unpredictable but nevertheless crucial—of the suitability of any particular analyst: "which analyst, for which patient?"[1]

The countertransference: at the heart of the analyst's work

Since the work of psychoanalysis requires that both protagonists participate in it, the implication is that this work cannot be properly carried out unless there is an active meeting of minds between them. This active meeting of minds working together produces interpretation, interpretative processing and working-through. Hence the importance for every analysis of the analyst's countertransference—which for some writers in fact precedes the transference proper (Neyraut, 1974)—defined traditionally as a series of unconscious reactions, in the analyst, to the patient as a person and more specifically to the patient's transference.

As analysts listen to their patients, they are caught up in the very essence of the transference movement that patients subject them to, and have to do some internal work on themselves (the "work of the counter-transference" (de Urtubey, 1994)). This work is helpful in that it enables analysts to get in touch with the difficulties they may be experiencing in dealing with certain types of material (for example, echoing their own repressed drive impulses), and it can help them to acquire a better understanding of the clusters of unconscious conflicts that the patient is coming up against in the transference. These now become meaningful, they can be interpreted and then restored to the patient.

Hence the countertransference, the "countering" resistance or counter-resistance, can become the source of the analyst's most productive intuitions; though also an obstacle, the countertransference should be regarded as one of the most valuable tools an analyst at work and through his or her work can hope to possess.

Interpretation

The work of interpretation creates a "space for play" (Winnicott, 1971) that is both intra- and inter-psychic. Interpretation enables repression to be lifted, memories to be recalled, affects to be liberated, and representations to be created; it is the psychoanalytic instrument par excellence, the very essence of the psychoanalytic process both for the analyst who thinks up an interpretation and puts it into words and for the patient who receives it and mulls it over. When it is processed, interpretation "simultaneously conveys, creates and rediscovers, it links desire, memory and insight" (Couvreur, 1991, p. 613); it enables the person who acknowledges it to accede to new levels of transformation and opens up fresh spaces in the mind. As a result, the patient can understand conflicts better and look on the functioning of his or her mind in a new way.

Always suspensive, never enigmatic, polysemous, open-ended, strategic or even tactical (de M'Uzan, 1988), connecting as closely as possible with the substance of the Preconscious and the psychoanalytic relationship, interpretation can produce a reconstruction that in itself is no more than a step forward or a temporary means of support; it may be taken up again, re-interpreted and subsequently worked on afresh. Interpretation, fruit of the psychoanalytic encounter, never comes to a close; it lies at the heart of the dialogue woven between the two protagonists of the analysis, which, once internalized, can go on more or less for ever, long after the analysis itself has come to an end.

Change and analysis

The work of the analysis gives the analysand an opportunity to make certain changes that encourage the development of new modes of mental functioning. In allowing access to the patient's own subjective position, these changes essentially involve modifying the patient's relationship with him- or herself. The capacity to look at oneself with an analytic eye increases awareness of certain repetitive automatisms at work since childhood and helps the patient overcome them; consequently, the destiny of affects and representations relating to desires involving the primary objects of childhood can also undergo considerable modification. Relationships between the patient and the demands of the superego, ego-ideal and ideal ego can, as a result, be made more flexible. It then becomes easier to accept the difference between the sexes and between generations; in other words, to acknowledge that the patient's own sex has its limits and that there exists another, different, sex. At the same time, the irreversible nature of time, the reality of death, the narcissistic wound linked to the existence of the Unconscious and the humiliation engendered by the untameable aspect of the id ... all these become easier to acknowledge. This implies accepting castration in all of its guises, including those that are expressed or stated in terms of separation; the result is greater freedom with respect to the life of the instinctual drives, including their erotic aspects, a heightened capacity for love and more openness in the direction of sublimation. To accomplish all this, the patient will have to tolerate the depressive pressures that in the end will prove helpful for coming to terms with past and future loss.

Thus, the hope that underlies every analysis is that one day the analysing function of the psychoanalyst can be introjected by the analysand; the end of an analysis is characterized by the fact that the patient can look upon him- or herself with some degree of detachment—the ability to be in closer touch with what is happening in the Unconscious. As René Diatkine puts it, the ability to stand back and achieve insight should have freed enough humour with respect to oneself and enough tenderness with respect to one's neighbour that life becomes more pleasant both for oneself and for others (Diatkine, 1988).

Note

1. As well as those concerning "why?" and "how?", when, on the analyst's side, resistances that could originally be moderated begin to organize themselves, with respect to the patient's material, at best as a countertransference neurosis and at worst as a negative "psychoanalytic" reaction.

CHAPTER FOUR

Clinical matters

In this chapter I report on three clinical cases that illustrate how transformations can occur in the patient's mind in the course of the psychoanalytic process and the work of the analysis.

With the first of these cases, I try to clarify how the work of the analysis can enable a patient to transform mental impulses, in particular through the analysis of the resistances relating to negative transference, and change how regression and repetition operate.

The short extract from the second analysis involves a particular kind of countertransference movement in the psychoanalyst when a traumatic event occurred in the patient's life that revived memories of earlier trauma in her past history.

The third analysis highlights the work of linking, un-linking and re-linking that the analyst has to accomplish when a patient finds him- or herself at a dead end as regards the capacity for representation. This dead-end emerges when the transference relationship unfolds without a sufficiently strong protective shield against stimuli, thereby giving rise to an overwhelming degree of eroticization.

Patrick: the fate of certain scars

Patrick consulted me some years ago now in order to disentangle the knots of a complex psychic situation, the consequence of compulsive acts that were completely blocking his sexuality and his love life. In addition, these acts were significant in that they led him to spend vast amounts of money—and each time they made him feel guilty and humiliated.

A graduate engineer of a prestigious college, Patrick was in his thirties. Many years before, he had left his family and the provincial town in which he had been brought up. An ambitious young man, with the means to achieve his ambitions and a highly successful professional career already in the making, Patrick none the less was very lonely in his emotional life (because of his personality, which he described as both touchy and difficult). In an attempt to put an end to his solitude, he had got into the habit—by then more and more compulsive—of meeting casual female partners who offered their services—for a fee—on the erotic viewdata network. His idea was to set up a threesome: two women plus himself. The distress he expressed as he described the ever more compulsive nature of these encounters, plus the guilt he felt at the depravity of this "neo-sexuality", led me to propose analysis even though I could see the risk of an underlying perverse structure that might weigh more or less heavily on the development of the psychoanalytic process. The deeply neurotic aspect of his throwing money down the drain in these nocturnal escapades, as well as two traumatic episodes that had had a considerable impact on his childhood, also encouraged me to think that Patrick would benefit from the analysis he desired.

His childhood, as I say, had been overshadowed by two traumatic events. An early trauma of which, on the conscious level, he was unaware, only took on its full force and became truly meaningful after some progress had been made in the analysis; a later trauma that had almost cost him his life was often used by Patrick as a tentative explanation of certain aspects of his behaviour. The elder of two children, Patrick had suffered his first trauma when his younger sister was born; he was no more than eleven months old at the time. According to Patrick, he would always subsequently treat his sister as if she were his twin. (The absence of any difference here underlines the emergence of counter-cathexis and perhaps even denial.) I could, therefore, suggest that for Patrick the birth of his sister had resulted at that point in a cruel feeling of loss with respect to his mother. The second trauma, in later childhood, occurred when he was about four years of age: he was playing a somewhat brutal game with his cousin when he fell into a tub of boiling water. He had third-degree burns over much of his body—only his head and face remained unscathed; he had to spend over a month in hospital in a germ-free atmosphere. His mother stayed with him, night and day, all the time he remained in hospital. He recovered after just a few weeks, a fact that, given the extent of his injuries and the initially reserved medical prognosis, astonished the physicians who were treating him. In the early stages of his analysis, we were able to suggest a reconstruction: one of the reasons for his recovering in such a short time was probably the fact that he was able in this fashion to have his mother all to himself again.

Apart from these traumatic events, Patrick's childhood and adolescence seem to have passed off fairly smoothly; he was brought up in the provinces, and at one point his family had been well-off—in the past, his paternal grandfather had been remarkably successful, both professionally and socially, to an extent well beyond what his modest background could have supposed. This grandfather was very much a patriarchal figure, authoritarian and feared. It was obvious that Patrick's father had neither the resolute personality nor the unbounded ambition of his own father—Patrick, in his own quiet but fierce way, never forgave him for that. As a result, Patrick's own ambition and professional success could be understood as a wish to repair the paternal image with respect to the grandfather figure; but above all they encapsulated elements of his rivalry with respect to his father. Therefore, it seemed quite clear that Patrick's financial problems—the consequence of his compulsive spending in connection with his sexual behaviour—were related to feelings of guilt over his aggressiveness towards the paternal imago and to his wish to reject it.

Though there was some suggestion that his preferred solutions to castration anxiety were perverse in nature, Patrick did seem to have tried, from adolescence on, to organize his life in such a way as to maintain the illusion of being in control over people and things—and even that he held them in his grasp. As a result, he made great use of defences whose anal-sadistic nature gave the impression of establishing a relatively inflexible obsessional neurosis. However, quite soon after the start of the analysis, it became apparent that an extremely active hysterical nucleus was hiding behind Patrick's neurotically obsessional character. When the hysterical aspect emerged, this "tortured soul"—it was almost as though he had been "burned alive"—would dramatize his relationships (as well as certain events which transported him away from his day-to-day existence) in a very theatrical manner. At times like these, the fragile nature of his narcissism, of his identifications, and even of his sense of identity were revealed as though in broad daylight.

In addition, Patrick was very unsure of himself. He would often worry when certain emotions emerged from within—he was never sure, in advance, whether he would be able to contain them and keep them under control. To protect himself in his relationships with other people, he had adopted a borrowed mental "cloak" that encouraged him to present an image of himself as someone extremely provocative and challenging—as he would often say to me, he wanted people to "feel afraid of him". It soon became obvious that presenting himself as someone unpredictable, cruel and even violent (and therefore dangerous) was related to the intense depressive anxiety Patrick had experienced ever since he was a young child. He did not succeed in counter-cathecting this anxiety other than through this kind of activity; it is easy to imagine that this simply made him feel all the more lonely and isolated. It was Patrick's way of verifying the authenticity of the link that people could establish with him, a link made up of demands that turned him into someone tyrannical and intolerable for his immediate circle. This was how he detected and tested other people's limits, so enabling him to verify his own: if he felt accepted by the Other, the Other, in turn, became acceptable to Patrick; if he could detect those limits, the Other, via identification, enabled Patrick to discover or to reinforce his own boundaries.

Negative paternal transference

It was in this climate of latent violence and constant threats to attack and even demolish the setting that the analysis began. Through his attempts to test the firmness and the boundaries of the analytic setting, Patrick was making sure of my firmness and my boundaries via the development of an unmistakable paternal transference whose negative pole was to remain very much to the fore for quite some time. In so doing, he was repeating the same provocative attitude he had displayed in the past with respect to his father in order to verify the latter's vigilance, firmness and authority. This was also Patrick's way of unconsciously reactivating in the present the conflict of authority between his grandfather, too authoritarian, and his father who, in Patrick's view, was not authoritarian enough. In Patrick's case, this conflict of authority was always transformed into a trial of strength; what was at stake here were the twin aspects, object-related and narcissistic, of obedience–insubordination/pride–humility.

In the first two years of the analysis, with his wish to make sure of his ability to control and take over the running of the treatment, Patrick attempted to manufacture a series of challenges for himself and to struggle against feelings of abandonment and passivity that were painfully reawakened in the transference with its manifest element of psychic homosexuality; he took some unconscionable risks that might have endangered not only the analysis but also his life.

For example, if he happened to be on a business trip to some distant town in the hour before the scheduled time of his session, he would in fact turn up at the correct time after driving all the way like a madman; he would tell me, with a triumphant feeling of having "cheated death", that, in order to do this, he had taken "as many risks as possible". The underlying fantasy was that of a phoenix rising from the ashes, thus highlighting the fact that each time Patrick tried to put himself in a situation bordering on the unacceptable he was eroticizing the memory he had of the accident that had occurred when he was four years old (falling into the tub of boiling water). His attitude of defiance and incredible risk-taking made me think of an unconscious suicidal attitude that often was to worry me; this changed, however, when I suggested that he was perhaps trying to show me all the efforts he was making for me and therefore how attached to me he really was. This transference interpretation enabled Patrick to build up a clearer representation of part of what was going on in his mind as regards the relationship developing between us and the cathexes it generated in him.

The interpretation helped us to analyse a defensive movement linked to the development of a positively-charged paternal transference. It thus acted as a container and as a protective shield, since it made sense of those actions of Patrick's that were putting him at risk. Created and put into words thanks to a transference–countertransference feeling (it should be remembered that I had good cause to be concerned, not to say worried), this kind of interpretation has nothing particularly exemplary about it. It is part of a whole series of interactions necessary for the creation of in-depth interpretative work—at times a backdrop of interpretation—of which the analysis of the transference forms the main vertex. It is this work of interpretation that enables certain rearrangements to be made in the patient's psychic economy via changes in the equilibrium and distribution of the small quantities of energy that come into play when cathexes and de-cathexes linked to the transference and to the work of the analysis are brought into operation.

Patrick had a very clear memory of his accident; he could describe it, image by image, like a film in slow motion. He would often explain to me how the very fact of storing the details of this event in memory and being able to break it down into separate sequences had enabled him to eradicate the recollection of the intense and long drawn-out pain of his burns, and split it off from that of the tremendous fear he and his family had experienced through the sheer drama of what had happened. This splitting, which he had maintained ever since, had also enabled him to transform, by counter-cathecting it, his mind-set as someone "burned alive" (the "tortured soul"). Converted into an apparent "shell of insensitivity"—and, at times, via projection, into a wish to inspire fear—this position then became an appeal addressed to his immediate circle or to his love objects for them to take on board his "pain" (i.e., the pain he had felt in the accident), which, at one swoop, incorporated, condensed and above all became the epitome of every other experience of mental pain.

Sometimes the eroticization of these states of mind went as far as to infiltrate the sessions. From time to time he would try to inflict pain on himself in a way that was supposed to remain hidden: later, he told me that when he squeezed the skin on his face between the nails of his thumb and forefinger, it was to experience anew the feeling of being burnt (in fact, his face had not been harmed at all in the accident). I had the impression that another aim of these actions—though he carried them out surreptitiously, over time I could not fail to notice what was going on—was to make me suffer, because all I could do was observe helplessly the attacks he was making on himself. I interpreted this to him. Later I was to enlarge on this interpretation, suggesting that this aspect of his behaviour in the sessions and its repetitiveness perhaps had two other meanings, both of which could be valid at the same time:

- on the one hand, in reawakening the memory of his past suffering related to the scalding accident, Patrick's idea was to set up a situation in which I would be wholly devoted to him, just as his mother had been when she had stayed all alone with him in the germ-free room;
- on the other, he was also trying to isolate and exclude me as his father had been after the accident by making me look helplessly on (just as his father had done) while his mother took care of him.

These interpretations enabled significant progress to be made in the analysis thanks to the prospect of creating meaningful representations of his various fantasy productions (Oedipal and primal scene) that alternated between combining and opposing, within himself, a "day baby" and a "(female) night lover", a "day mother" and a "night baby" (Braunschweig & Fain, 1975). As a result, some aspects of Patrick's material changed significantly. Though he had hardly ever spoken of his dreams before, he now began reporting a certain number that enabled us to analyse his negative transference; also, whereas the sheer force of his affects linked to the quantity of excitation aroused by our relationship used to be overwhelming, it now became more manageable, less intense and therefore more contained.

The analysis of repetition

The backdrop to these developments was that Patrick continued to wonder about his nocturnal and venal escapades in the course of which he gave free rein to his fantasy of being with two women at once—two women over whom he tried to exert absolute control via a scenario that involved them in homosexual intercourse. As the analysis progressed, it became more and more obvious that Patrick's irresistible need to set up this kind of meeting could be related to various unconscious feelings he had in the transference with respect to me: for example, he became depressed and resentful towards me when any kind of difficulty emerged, or when there were breaks in the analysis due to absence on my part.

These nocturnal escapades made him feel very guilty and led him sometimes to ask me to adopt an attitude of prohibition, punishment, and coercion with him. One day, at the end of a session entirely taken up with the questions these scenarios raised in his mind, Patrick heard the patient I was to see after him come into the waiting-room. He exclaimed: "Ah! It's nice to know a girl's coming in after me!" "A girl," I stressed, just then realizing that, via this fantasy, Patrick was continuing the kind of scenario he had just been talking to me about. The idea obviously was, as in his infancy, to form a group of three: his mother (represented by me), his sister (the "girl" who had just come into the waiting-room) and himself. I thereupon suggested an interpretation concerning what he was repeating when he set up these erotic threesomes: to bring under his absolute control and domination what he had in the past experienced as a true narcissistic wound, that is, looking on in fascination as his mother took care of his sister, without being able to do anything about it, and feeling excluded. Each time he reported these escapades, he was trying to make me experience the exclusion he had felt in the past—by drawing me into these adventures in the hope that they would excite and fascinate me, he was trying to make me feel the helplessness mingled with rage he himself had experienced in his childhood. It was also a reminder that once again I was put in the same position as his father who, excluded from the germ-free room during Patrick's hospitalization, could only look on helplessly as the mother took care of the son.

As a result of these interpretations, a certain number of modifications began to appear almost imperceptibly in Patrick's life and in his mental functioning. As to changes in his life-style, two facts in particular were significant: on the one hand, he had less and less need to have recourse to venal affairs, and, on the other, he met a young woman and fell in love with her. They decided to live together.

Given the link between states of mind and repetition, it is the interpretation of repetition in the transference that enables us to hope that, in the long term, there will be some degree of change in the analysand's psychic economy and functioning. In "Remembering, repeating and working-through", Freud writes:

> [. . .] the patient repeats instead of remembering, and repeats under the conditions of resistance. [. . .] we must treat his illness, not as an event of the past, but as a present-day force. This state of illness is brought, piece by piece, within the field and range of operation of the treatment, and while the patient experiences it as something real and contemporary, we have to do our therapeutic work on it, which consists in a large measure in tracing it back to the past. [Freud, 1914g, pp. 151–152]

A little further on, he adds:

> The main instrument, however, for curbing the patient's compulsion to repeat and for turning it into a motive for remembering lies in the handling of the transference. [. . .] We regularly succeed in giving all the symptoms of the illness a transference meaning and in replacing his ordinary neurosis with a "transference-neurosis" of which he can be cured by the therapeutic work. [*ibid.*, p. 154]

This extract makes it very clear what Freud believed to be the essence of the analyst's work, and in particular of interpretation, as regards the various transference tendencies which originate in the compulsion to repeat and attempt to carry through into the analysis. The transference neurosis, as the motive force behind psychoanalysis, reactivates memory traces liked to the development of infantile sexuality and the Oedipus complex, it puts the patient through the same set of wounds and scars that were there originally, and it reawakens painful feelings from the past relating to wrongs, loss of love, and loss of self-esteem. The transference neurosis is therefore both a source of progress (on its development depends the whole psychoanalytic process) and a source of resistance. In the latter case, it opposes any change, since remembering does not always prevent the effects of same and identical from being repeated (de M'Uzan, 1969).

We know also that repetition does not involve simply an unquenchable thirst for wish-fulfilment. "Beyond the pleasure principle" taught us that the compulsion to repeat is produced also by the formation of a protective shield against stimuli in order to reduce the excitation generated as a consequence of trauma. Given the need to control some forms of excitation—relating to traumatic traces—we could suggest that the compulsion to repeat does not involve merely reviving and controlling but can also be seen as displacing and perhaps reactivating excitation via fantasy representation.

This indeed seems to be the way that a certain part of the organization and impact of Patrick's compulsion to repeat functioned. My comments and interpretations directly relating to the development of the psychoanalytic process were brought about by the repetition of the fantasy activity consequent on the organization of his trauma and their traces in perception and memory. With these interpretations, I began to emphasize the crucial elements that participated in the metaphorical reconstruction of the central fantasy behind his version of the primal scene: observing intercourse between two women, his mother and his sister, in a homosexual relationship that more or less fused them together, connected with nursing care of the body; given that he felt physically and mentally excluded from the situation, this excited him, tortured him, burned him alive, made him furious and despairing, depressed him and, to cap it all, made him feel confused. To defend himself against this state of confusion, Patrick used the splitting mechanisms I have mentioned to separate the representation of the trauma (producing fear, as we have seen) from the affect of intense pain related to it.

Fear of a child, desire for a child

A significant change in Patrick's states of mind occurred once it became possible to represent and to verbalize how he imagined the primal scene.

Speaking of his new partner, now that they had decided to live together, Patrick was in a complaining mood: "She's 'heavy' and 'hot'," he said, and that worried him. She reminded him too much of the "matron-like" women he knew as a boy—his mother, a stoutish woman, and his maternal grandmother. He complained of feeling passive and child-like—she was the one who took all the initiatives when they were making love. He was fascinated by her stomach; it attracted him but at the same time he felt it repellent. He reported a dream: one of his fingers seemed to be swollen; there was a bulge on it, like a blister. He could see a worm crawling out of it; he felt disgust at the sight. He associated to the ambivalence he felt towards his new boss, who was ambitious, demanding, efficient, and as unsentimental as anyone could be—the kind of ideal image that Patrick had wanted to cultivate. Patrick had become the boss's right-hand man; he gave me to understand that his boss was more or less the same age as I was. On the one hand, Patrick was delighted to see in his boss some of his own conceptions, but on the other he was afraid to lose part of his independence and the kind of hold he had had over his previous boss. From now on he would have to "show what he was made of".

At that point in his associations, he came back to the dream and the two elements in it that intrigued him most: the swelling/blister on his finger, and the repugnant and disgusting worm he saw crawl out of it. He thought of women menstruating and of the uneasiness he felt whenever he saw a pregnant woman. Swelling, blister, burns, stomach, bulging, "bun in the oven", "worm-child", menstruation were all signifiers that evoked the fantasy of pregnancy (with anal connotations) as though, in the session, they formed a series of signposts at the junction of several contradictory or complementary currents of Patrick's fears and desires.

In the following session, Patrick, who seemed very anxious, was hardly on the couch before he uttered a loud "Shit!" and punched the side-cushion with his fist. After a somewhat paralysed silence as a result of this violence, his associations made it clear that it was me whom Patrick wanted to punch, and, through me, his new boss. With respect to some of his previous material, I had in my mind the fantasy that he was punching a pregnant woman in the stomach in order to cause a miscarriage. This was in part confirmed when he told me that he had felt extremely anxious all day, because he had had sex with his partner without using a condom.

At that point, the whole of Patrick's material, with the dream as its fulcrum, could be read in its true transference dimension:

- the swollen-burnt finger and the blister had to do with the burning aspect of his transference as a "tortured soul";
- the disgusting worm that crawled out of the finger—the worm of a rotting apple—represented the child he feared his partner (and through her, his mother) desired and expected from the father;
- the worm also expressed his disgust and his fear that, in identification with his mother's desires with respect to the father, his own unmentionable wish to have a child from his boss (both the new one and the former one), i.e. from me, might suddenly surface;
- the worm was a condensed image of his wish to give his mother a baby and the resultant castration anxiety;
- the exclamation "shit!" that burst forth in the following session with the violent punch at the cushion could be seen as an unsuccessful defensive manoeuvre against the reappearance of the disgusting worm-representation of the dream—this brought him back to the feelings of depression and helplessness that had overwhelmed him when he was confronted with his sister's conception and subsequent birth;
- the exclamation could also evoke the terror and anxiety he felt as he fell into the tub of boiling water when he was four years old. He could no longer evacuate these feelings as he had done in the past by setting up splitting mechanisms to hive them off.

Shortly after this, after having broken off his relationship with his friend (they were back together again a few weeks later), Patrick analysed the fact that he could not bear the feeling she gave him of expecting him to be loving and tender towards her. This brought him face to face, for the first time in his analysis, with the fact that, as a child, he could not stand his mother showing affection towards him—indeed, he went as far as to forbid her from making any kind of demonstration of this kind. One day, he had a clash at work with one of the secretaries—she burst into tears—and he came into his session very upset. He said he could not bear to see a woman cry because he was afraid of identifying with her, losing his self-control and have swelling up inside him the feelings of distress he had experienced in the past when he saw women in his immediate circle, and in particular his mother, in tears. Patrick told me at that point that he had known, even as a very young child—he was only two months old!—that his mother had cried for *several days on end when she learned she was pregnant with his sister.*

The regressive path

In this particular phase of the analysis, Patrick's fear of his passive wishes became manifest—this was later to prove a defining moment of change for him. The regressive path he followed, starting with the dream, was the stimulus for a significant change in the way his mind functioned, and enabled him to gain insight into the conflicts he came up against; these related to a condensation of his own sexual desires and an identification he felt to be shameful with his mother's sexual desires—which, in addition, he confused with her desire for motherhood.

The connection that emerges when tentative movement is transformed into real change (the shift from movement to change with respect to mental functioning) involves both the work the mind has to do under the aegis of the compulsion to repeat and that which is dependent on the regression–progression polarity. In other words, no analysis of repetition is possible other than through the kind of work that requires regression—and vice-versa: regression (formal, topographical, temporal and libidinal) creates the conditions that make analysis of repetition possible.

Given the limitations imposed on perception and motor activity, together with the establishment of the setting—the fundamental rule, the psychoanalyst's silence as backdrop, the rhythm of the sessions—the analytic situation, with the transference manifestations it produces, encourages regression, especially topographical regression. Consequently, the analyst becomes the person and the locus for receiving the transference of the relationship between the patient and his or her internal objects; the transference is an expression of the link between the child within the patient and the present-day adult, and between the child and the adults he or she was dependent on—that is, between the child in the patient and his or her internal objects.[1]

From the patient's point of view, this regressive situation is both wished-for and feared: the wish to be in a situation of dependence, together with the anxiety associated both with the relaxing of controls over what comes from within and with threats from without. Associated with certain representations of affect and the fantasies relating to them, anxiety is the sign that this regressive move is being resisted.

As Cosnier points out, in spite of the difference in roles, shared topographical regression enables restoration of what in the past the patient missed out on in the adult–child relationship: adult identification with the child's wishes and affects, enabling them to be linked together by means of words (Cosnier, 1992).

When, as in Patrick's case, there has been pain and distress (trauma) in childhood that overwhelm the defence mechanisms, the transference neurosis, in so far as it manifests the effects of regression, can be held up for quite some time because of the anxiety it entails. Drive impulses are more easily expressed in external relationships, such as lateral transference, because the confrontation with reality is much more reassuring. This crucial kind of defence against transference reactivation may lead to violent attacks turned back against the patient or to other types of expression—enactment, maladjusted behaviour, persecution.

Transference manifestations cannot be reduced to their simple repetitive function—they are also innovative and creative. It is not simply a return to the same situation as in the past. As Gibeault points out, the idea of temporal regression in analysis, with its twin poles of narcissism and object relations, enables integration of passivity and receptivity, both of which are indispensable for the experience of mankind (Gibeault, 1992).

In this sense, when we try to predict whether or not a prospective patient is suitable for analysis, we have to take into account his or her capacity for tolerating regression without loss of boundaries. When Freud spoke of the "underlying biological bedrock" as an obstacle to change, he was trying to account for the obstacles that lie in the path of the capacity to internalize, in a containing manner, femininity and primary receptivity. In "Analysis terminable and interminable", Freud described these as resistances from the id (1937c, pp. 238–239) and as a denial of femininity in both sexes.

Marie: a state of "emergency"

The short extract that I am about to present illustrates a phase in the course of an analysis in which the analyst's countertransference was brought into play much more directly than is usually the case. The fact that my countertransference was aroused in this way meant that I was able to throw some light on one aspect of the conflict situation that was being played out on the patient's mental stage.

> Marie was a young woman who came to analysis in order to liberate herself from certain impressions she had retained from her childhood. She had been subjected to a whole series of traumatic events (which I shall not go into here), one of the most serious being her father's long-unsuspected but nevertheless severe heart condition. The fact that he had to be placed under constant medical surveillance meant that the threat of an "emergency" that might suddenly erupt at any time of day or night was continually hanging over the family.
>
> Marie was the elder of two children; she was eight years old and her younger brother six when her father fell ill. Marie's father was a very gentle but also very anxious man, who could at times be extremely violent; Marie was very upset every time any such violence occurred in her presence—she had the impression she was the root cause of it all. The fact that she had a memory of her father as an affectionate person in her infancy led her to believe that his angry and violent behaviour began as a result of his heart trouble. Though she had been able to analyse at some length the fact that her father's verbal violence, at times targeted at her, hid his very real tenderness towards and attachment to her, she did feel hurt and wounded each time.
>
> Marie described her mother as a "robust" but somewhat inflexible woman; Marie had all the more difficulty in putting up with this inflexibility since her mother had become for her, as for the rest of the family, a highly idealized model.
>
> In spite of the conflict situations that Marie's complex relationships with her parents had generated, she was still very attached to them. The masochistic links she had developed with respect to her parental imagos had become the model for the other relationships she had established during adolescence and adulthood; these in fact had caused many of the problems about which she consulted me.
>
> In the first session of the short sequence I shall now report, Marie spoke of a brief trip abroad with her parents. During this brief holiday, her father on several occasions had been verbally violent towards her;

Marie found his behaviour even more difficult to put up with because he gave her the impression that he was using his heart condition to blackmail her, claiming that he felt physically unwell—even though he seemed the picture of health.

After reporting these elements and saying that they saddened her, Marie—unusually for her—did not go on to develop the complex melancholy feeling her father's attitude towards her ordinarily gave rise to. Thinking of what she had called "blackmail", she said for the first time that if in the past he had succumbed to his illness—as well might have been the case at times—she might at present be suffering less than she was; this was partly because since his illness her father's attitude meant that she had mixed feelings towards him—ambivalence would be putting it mildly—and this she could no longer tolerate. Thus, she expressed the idea that if her father had died while she was still a child, his death might not have had the catastrophic impact on her she had always imagined. She spent some time toying with this idea, which was new to her; she was surprised it hadn't occurred to her sooner. She interrupted what she was saying to mention that ever since she'd taken up the topic, she'd done nothing else but think of her death wishes towards her father, aroused by his recent angry and hurtful words. Up until that moment, these death wishes had never seemed so clear to her as they proved to be in this session; her growing awareness of them meant that there now opened up before her the possibility of freeing herself from certain masochistic attitudes she manifested with respect to her father. The session ended with her astonishment and quasi-euphoria at the idea of having been able to think along these lines so freely.

I shall not spend time going into all the latent thoughts implied by Marie's words. I had the feeling they could account for the many versions of the Oedipal drama that Marie was playing out on her mental stage, thanks to the transference relationship (in particular her death wishes with respect to me as her analyst). I had in mind the idea that, for her, what was being played out had to do with the fact that ever since childhood she had unconsciously experienced her father's illness as the only companionship he had (in other words, Marie had felt that his illness was her only true rival).

In a state of shock

The next day, Marie phoned me at the time her session was scheduled to begin. She was in tears and, as a result, it was difficult to make out what she was saying. I understood that she was unable to come for her session; I could make out, between the sobs that made communication difficult, something like "hospitalized ... my father ... no hope ...". I had the impression she was telling me that her father had been hospitalized, that there was "no hope" for him and that she had to go to the hospital to be with her mother. Though unable to make any more sense of what she was saying, I sympathized with her and understood (or, perhaps, surmised) that she was trying to see if she could have another session at a different time that day; I therefore suggested an appointment that very evening, which she immediately accepted.

When I went to greet Marie for this replacement session, I found her in a daze, a state of mental paralysis that immediately made me think of a traumatic "state of shock" ... I was therefore on the alert, but at the same time quite puzzled. Marie was hardly on the couch before she curled up in a foetus-like position, something that, for her, was unusual. She told me that when she had phoned me earlier in the day, she had just received a phone call from her mother to say that her father, whose state of health had not seemed particularly alarming, had nevertheless been rushed to hospital for an "emergency" check-up and that when her younger brother had learned of this he had had a car accident—so that he too had been rushed, as an emergency case, to the casualty department.

"Stop," moaned Marie, "it's all too much for me to handle! My mother sends me an SOS and wants me to help her, my father's in hospital, my brother's in no great shape and I'll have to take care of him too ... Will they never leave me alone!"

She was in a state of near-collapse, she felt she was at the end of her tether ... She did not want to have to deal with all that, taking care of them and feeling herself regarded simply as an extension of her mother. The accumulation of traumatic events took her back to those of her childhood, overwhelming her ... she felt exhausted. Then she fell silent for a long time.

In my countertransference, I felt very sympathetic towards her despair. I therefore decided to say something at once. I tried to relate her present experience to the encroachment of reality on fantasy, with regard to the sudden parallelism between what she had told me in the previous session (the idea of death wishes against her father and the feeling of quasi-euphoria she had mentioned) and the news she had received that day, which brought back memories of past catastrophes.

I had the impression that the state of distress into which Marie suddenly found herself plunged—the result of too close a fit between her internal world (the recent recalling of one aspect of her wishes) and the external world of physical reality—had had the immediate effect of provoking a real collapse of her inner topography (Janin, 1996). Marie no longer knew where she stood: there was, as it were, a blurring of the dividing line between internal and external, and a confusion between psychic reality and external reality.

Marie was experiencing the situation as a series of catastrophic "emergencies" that brought back to her mind certain traumatic memories from the past; her response to this was to dramatize the situation and generate a psychic "emergency" (the result of "too much for her to handle" breaking through her protective shield and plunging her into a state of deep distress).

I could partly understand this state of affairs, yet I felt somewhat disconcerted by the mental paralysis and distress that Marie manifested. I was confronted with an aspect of Marie the existence and importance of which I had never imagined until then; I felt quite concerned, not to say deeply worried.

After this replacement session, Marie's distress vanished; in fact she quickly realized that her father's state of health, as well as that of her brother, did not give cause for concern. As a result, I felt less worried about her—but more and more puzzled because, in the sessions that followed, a remarkable state of negativity developed between us. This was something new, and manifested itself as silent hostility that, though unvoiced, was no less intense. That situation—described by Marie as painful for her, and which in my countertransference I experienced as stressful—was to last for several weeks.

Marie missed none of her sessions during all those weeks; she was none the less convinced that all she could express was her hostility towards me. Completely shut off and silent, she said she felt "scraped clean". Thanks to some of the comments I made, there gradually appeared in the background the idea that she could not forgive me for having allowed her fantasies concerning her death wishes towards her father to break through into broad daylight. Ever since then she had had the feeling—she admitted that it was undoubtedly projective—that "everybody", including me, reproached her for even contemplating that kind of thought, and she felt "shattered" by that idea. This situation lasted for several sessions, until a certain degree of insight enabled me to grasp the state of mind that Marie had been in for some time past.

Seduction and the countertransference

In this session, Marie again took up the theme of her father's recent hospitalization and the difficulty she had been having with me ever since. In addition to the persecutory thoughts we had talked about, there was the idea that throughout the recent events she had not felt as "up to it all" as her mother would have been—she had not been able to come to her scheduled session, but she had had to make sure I would tolerate the fact that she could ask for "emergency" help; and I had indeed done so, instead of "sending her packing until her next session", as she put it. She couldn't stop thinking that ever since then I've been rebuking her for this; she felt ashamed and discredited. From now on, she said, she would like to keep "as far away from me as possible".

I repeated: "As far away from me as possible?"

Marie replied: "Yes, like when I came for my extra session, when I tried to settle down on the couch as far away as possible from you . . . curled up like a foetus."

This threw fresh light on the situation in which Marie and I had found ourselves. What she had just said made it more meaningful: the fact that I had accepted the replacement session—or was it not rather the case that I had myself suggested it?—had been experienced by Marie as an attempt on my part to seduce her.

Consequently, a certain number of questions concerning what, in my countertransference, had driven me to suggest—or to accept—the additional session flocked into my mind: what had led me to act in the countertransference? What was the "demand" that I had found intolerable, to such an extent that I had probably transformed it into an "emergency"? Who was the reparatory demon I had thereupon succumbed to? In that situation, whose place had I usurped? To what kind of unconscious "seduction" on Marie's part had I given in? All these questions crowded into my mind, but at that point I had no answer to any of them—until I heard, as an echoing association, the words Marie had uttered in the session: "curled up like a foetus", reminding me of the part that guides the firing-pin on a gun;[2] I could then see that my countertransference impulse might have had something to do with the theme Marie had been discussing in the session that preceded the events that led me to suggest the extra session—her death wish concerning her father and, in the transference, myself. In a certain sense, I had "jumped the gun".

I was then forced to recognize that I had counter-cathected Marie's attitude towards her father—I had felt that I was the target of the gun/ "hammer of a rifle"; even though the rifle was not consciously present as far as I was concerned, I probably had the feeling and the fear that Marie was about to take aim! I then hurriedly transformed my counter-cathexis into a reparative movement by agreeing to (or proposing to) offer her the substitute session.

But perhaps my countertransference reparative movement was aimed at repairing not only Marie but also myself as a parental image (both paternal and maternal) under rifle attack from the negative transference.

The "hammer of a gun" called to mind also the foetal position in which Marie might find herself again if her father had died—she would then have been with me as a mother-figure in the transference, hence her attempt to keep me "as far away as possible" from her.

Did I have to go on thinking—as I had done in the initial stages of my analysis of the countertransference movement—that I had been in the position of a "seducer seduced by the emergency", in order to defend myself against being in one that gave me the impression I was just as likely to be castrated as Marie's father?

The fact that my thinking had followed that particular path might perhaps have involved something in Marie that had to do with the idea of "seduction by emergency". In the past, she had been subjected to that kind of seduction via sexual fantasies in which life and death were mixed up, due to her father's illness having subsequently become highly eroticized; a state of stupor and mental paralysis might have been one of the negative forms in which this seduction was expressed.

I was then able to understand her silently negative and hostile attitude as an illustration of what Freud had written concerning the transference: "transference to the doctor is suitable for resistance to the treatment only in so far as it is a negative transference or a positive transference of repressed erotic impulses" (Freud, 1912b, p. 105).

Marie and I were thereupon both able to become aware of the importance of that eroticization in her transference to me and of the dramatizing impact it had.

Samuel: the sinking of the Titanic

One day in the course of his analysis, Samuel exclaimed: "This will not be the Wailing Wall of my premature ejaculation!"

Some years before, this young man had indeed sought analysis for this symptom, which haunted him. He had dreaded it ever since adolescence, and experienced it as shameful, a deficiency in his functioning, a narcissistic wound—just as he felt his need for analysis to be. His request for a consultation and subsequently for analysis was related mainly to this symptom, with no other apparent psychological problems to complain of.

Samuel was in his thirties, unmarried and highly intelligent; he had a promising job with a well-known firm. All this, in his view, was in stark contrast to his sex life, which he felt was mediocre and lacking in interest given his symptom and the "excitability" associated with it.

The distress this caused Samuel, the related neurotic symptoms, and his past history—in particular the death of his father in a car accident when Samuel was thirteen—argued in favour of my accepting him for analysis.

A certain number of themes were gone into quite quickly, in particular Samuel's need, from adolescence onwards, to set up transvestite scenarios (using undergarments he stole from the women in his immediate circle) as an accompaniment to masturbation, as well as the irresistible urge to empty his bowels every time he felt anxious (he would tactfully refer to this as his "scatological problem"). In addition, I began to experience a certain number of feelings:

- that he was coming to his sessions more in order to find a means, thanks to a comforting presence, of enabling him to master and control his premature ejaculation than in order to show any real interest in what his mind could produce and how this could develop within the psychoanalytic relationship. As a result, he always spoke of "curing" his symptom as the aim of the analysis;
- that for Samuel his childhood began when his father died. In this way, he was attempting to do away with the past, both his own and that of his family, and any memories he still had of it. In setting more store by what was happening in the present, he gave the impression that it was particularly difficult for him to admit that he had had a childhood, that he had indeed been a child and that as a result he may well have developed at one point or another an infantile neurosis.

Nevertheless, it was at once obvious in the analysis that his problems relating to over-cathexis of auto-erotic activity and the influence it had on his mental functioning not only offered but in fact provided an immediate transcription of what was to be the core theme of the analysis during the many years it lasted. A certain number of factors linked to his commitment to the analysis very quickly enabled me to stress the importance, both as regards symbolic content and as signifiers, of two crucial terms (and themes): emptiness and running away. These were to be at the centre of our work together because they circumscribed and defined the boundaries that Samuel imposed on the analysis and on me as his analyst. Among other things, it was the ability to make a connection between these two terms that helped Samuel to build up and consolidate over time mental representations—or a series of mental representations—sufficiently cathected to modify the way his mind functioned on the economic and topographical levels.

Pregenital anxiety

Faced with the fear of regressive and passive fantasies aroused by the psychoanalytic situation, Samuel never failed to eroticize, in the sessions, his experience of being narcissistically wounded and castrated. Whatever the moment, whatever the theme, he would talk about the sexual limitations his symptom forced on him, complaining about it and saying how distressed it made him feel. At the same time, from the very beginning of the analysis, Samuel would use up a considerable amount of energy to push to the fore certain elements of his perverse polymorphous sexuality that revolved, *inter alia*, around complicated fetishist rituals. In his eyes, they were useful as exorcisms and represented his attempts to cure himself of his symptom. But, that aside, they reflected above all his uncertainty and extreme identificatory confusion, reawakened and highlighted by the analytic situation. That situation worried him all the more since his bisexuality and the work connected with it—or, rather, with its failures—were constantly called into question by the analysis.

I would consistently find myself referred by him to these various issues in which his narcissistic wounds, his identificatory problems, and his castration anxiety (anal as well as genital) were all the time entangled; as such, I was invariably subjected to a never-ending barrage of harassment—"I want you to say something to me, to explain . . . I want you to take a more leading role, to be more focused . . .". Whole sessions were often like that, with a whirlwind atmosphere that completely exhausted me. The countertransference was all the more uncomfortable in that this was Samuel's way of "emptying" or "draining" himself of all thinking: he came to the sessions to "empty" himself, like an echo of the irresistible intestinal "draining" he felt coming over him whenever he found himself in a situation he experienced as anxiety-arousing.

One of the best examples of the "uncanny" and confused situations he found himself in at that time was when he invented the term "female vagina"; he used it constantly at the beginning of the analysis to designate the area in women that he dreaded since it carried with it some of Samuel's most terrifying fantasies. I found myself asking him one day, in passing, "the female vagina, as opposed to the male one, do you mean?" This helped us to uncover an identificatory fantasy in which a "male vagina"—anal, dry, empty and as such devoid of anything worrying or dangerous—was contrasted with a "female vagina"—a wet, dirty and dangerous thing that had to be hidden by white panties. The panties and their whiteness then became "exciting", as he put it. This made me think of an oral, anal, and genital telescoping, because on to this "female vagina" was projected a whole series of fantasies concerning the destructiveness of his penis, in danger of being "caught up" in this vagina, "bitten", "macerated", then faecalized.

In this way, Samuel's pregenital aspects showed how he considered himself to be in danger of being violently caught up in an anal backwash, a fixation point laden with poorly-contained conflicts relating above all to the sadism he attributed to his mother. They were the depository of horrifying faecalization fantasies involving a possessive and envious mother, thereby adding a new dimension to his confusion. The intensity of these faecalization fantasies brought his anxiety to a climax, in particular when combined with castration anxiety. As a result, as on many other occasions, Samuel eroticized the situation and tried to drag—or engulf—us both down inside the faecalization process which, at that point, was engulfing him. He wanted me to say something so that he could grasp at my comments; but whenever I did say something, he experienced it as a faecal penis that had first to be evacuated then immediately replaced.

With his obvious difficulty in containing and processing certain representations, Samuel ran away from intrapsychic conflict and plunged into action. Many times, faced with too high a level of excitation and finding it impossible to bind or defer them in order to make them more acceptable to his state of mind, Samuel fled the analysis, the analyst and his projections involving them. He would "vacate the premises". He stopped coming to sessions—absences that sometimes lasted for two or three weeks; he literally "vanished into thin air" in order to make me experience the emptiness his absence created, the same emptiness he himself had felt after the death of his father, I surmised. This attitude often weighed on the analysis, and an atmosphere of potential breakdown in the transference constantly hovered over our work; his threats to leave me echoed to some extent those of his latest woman friend who, according to Samuel, felt sexually frustrated by him and therefore no longer wanted to stay with him. These attacks on the setting, related to his difficulty in containing and thinking through certain representations, illustrated the kind of relationship Samuel had with his internal objects, as well as their position and the qualities attributed to them.

Paternal transference

The situation, then, was that Samuel was very obviously asking me to support him with my "interpretating penis", and this gave him the impression of being able to avoid being caught up in a series of engulfing and confusing representations that systematically confronted him with the "maternal hole"; the paternal transference quickly became established.

The first steps towards integrating the paternal transference were based on the apparent lack of (or, at least, difficulty with) anal introjection of the paternal penis. This acted as a counterpoint to the situation into which he tried constantly to lock us both: either he would put me in the position of someone who remained silent in the background (in his eyes, I became the equivalent of an anal-sadistic, greedy, demanding, and castrating woman or mother), or he would put me in the position of someone who gave into him by responding to some of his endless requests for me to say something. I then became a weak person who agreed to his slightest whim, like his father in the past.

Through his associations, it gradually became clear that I was to be the "rudder that he himself did not have in his stern"; his impression was that his father had not been able to fulfil that role for him. Later, he would even fantasize that, protected by my reassuring presence behind him (with the suggestion of anally introjecting my penis), he could more easily make love to a woman.

These positive attitudes with respect to me contrasted with the discredited image he gave of his father—until then, Samuel had tried in vain to idealize him; idealization was all the more important for him in that it had begun as a result of his father's sudden death.

At least twice in the past his father had "fallen" in Samuel's eyes—first through his reputation in the family as a "nonentity". He had had no ambition to get on in life, had been too self-effacing and had never managed to assert himself or impose his views on anybody. The second time was when he quite literally did fall, the day of the fatal car accident . . . It was long after the analysis had begun that Samuel told me his father had drowned in his car after it had fallen over a cliff as a result of the accident.

In keeping back this detail for so long Samuel had tried to make it seem insignificant. This showed just how important were the consequences of the huge traumatic impact Samuel had experienced at the time; as an after-effect, many traces were subsequently to be found in the analysis in relation to his defences and his attempts at integration.

From time to time the analysis seemed to him to be a journey inside himself that would enable him, as he was winding his way along (along the road where his father had had the fatal accident), to get in touch with the father whose absence Samuel experienced as a void that had to be filled; this came as a tremendous surprise to him. In addition, the dream he reported at that point was also a surprise: Samuel was making love, containing himself (i.e., not ejaculating prematurely) because he had two penises combined into one. One for urinating, the other for ejaculating. This dream made me think that in his childhood Samuel had probably been enuretic, though nothing of the sort had as yet come up in the analysis. His associations could be construed as "a penis for urinating"—his—and "one for ejaculating"—mine—or vice-versa, but in any case mine combined with his (the child's penis combined with the father's), thereby enabling him both to contain himself and to feel contained by me.

The story of the father's discovery of an exchange of correspondence between Samuel as a young adolescent and another boy of his age was a watershed in his awareness of what was at stake in the relationship with me. In this exchange of tender letters, there appeared fantasies and daydreams, the homosexual content of which was obvious. Samuel's father wanted to discuss this with him, but came up against a categorical refusal—"running away"—on his son's part. This fragment from the past enabled us to relate the latent thoughts that Samuel had about me each time he "ran away" from me to those he had avoided in the past by running away from his father. He set up an "emptiness", an "absence", in order to protect himself against homosexual fantasies, the fear of his passive wishes and castration anxiety with respect to me. This ostensibly offered him some degree of protection against primitive conflicts, the "emptiness" he himself experienced, and the fear of losing the boundaries of his self every time he was faced with feminine identifications—for example, whenever the topic came up in the sessions.

"Waves and wavering . . ."

Samuel's excitability, however, knew no bounds, and this worried him a great deal.

Whether it was a dream the associations to which led him along unknown paths, forgetting someone's name, a slip of the tongue, a comment or interpretation that I suggested to him—everything was turned into a reason for and an object of erotogenic representations because he over-cathected auto-erotic activity. As a result, the precarious equilibrium he had established between wishes and defences was rapidly short-circuited. At exhausting and "emptying" moments like those, experienced as such both by Samuel and by me, I had the impression that some kind of direct erotic enacting was taking place; their auto-erotic origin encouraged all sorts of narcissistic cathexes, especially those involving the body, that were rooted in a more positive image of his body and the exchanges he had with it.

In contrast to the fundamental nature of bisexuality, implying a relationship with two objects contained in the same psychic envelope, where the essence of the phallus is to be the object that passes through (Caïn, 1977), in Samuel it was his own body that he cathected as a love object. This was his way of saying that, even in the presence of his analyst, for him there was only one subject related to only one object—himself.

This often gave me the impression of a very strange clinical situation, close to what Gillibert (1977) has described as auto-erotic insanity. In these character neuroses difficult to systematize—undoubtedly severe and worrying, they often have a strong hint of phobia or of powerful hypochondriac anxieties—we can very quickly find ourselves plunged into a mental universe dominated by the fact that the entire internal body space becomes erotogenic: everything is experienced as sexual, sexualizable, sexualized, and therefore terrifying. Thinking itself becomes a stepping-stone to erotogeneity, something that, if not already erotogenic, can easily become so—it therefore becomes a persecutory element because of the over-excitability it can engender at such times.

In a series of embarrassed questions, Samuel wondered about my silence and my abstention from making any comments; he said that he "could not stand the idea that, in the sessions, I would make him think of his own wavering aspect . . .". It became obvious in the comments he made about this complaint that he wanted me to forbid him to continue with his fetishist activity. When I said this to him, he agreed. He then associated to prohibitions and castration, and mentioned the truss his father used to wear—and which continued to intrigue Samuel. We were then able to relate "women's panties" to this "truss". After making this link—which, at the time, Samuel saw as surprising—he was again afraid that I would fall silent once more. I reminded him that he had just told me of a similar fear when he seemed to be dreading the emergence of a "wavering" aspect . . .

"'Wavering' makes me think of waves, and the sinking of the *Titanic*. I saw the film when I was a boy," he said. "Women and children first! They were saved thanks to the lifeboats. Since there wasn't enough room for everybody, the menfolk stayed on the liner and went down with it. But what impressed me above all in the film was the story of the man who dressed up as a woman in order to get into a lifeboat and save his life . . ."

"Floating on the waves, 'wave-ring', means saving your life—maybe this is possible only if you're disguised as a woman?" I asked.

"'Wavering' could have something to do with being a woman? That idea worries me, like all the waves that threaten me." This was when, for the first time, Samuel thought of telling me about the enuresis that had so disturbed his nights as a child.

Lifting the silence (denial) about this—linked to the shameful experience, for Samuel, of having wet his bed as a child—enabled us gradually to build up a history of his parents. Because of the Shoah (Holocaust), several members of his mother's family had disappeared in circumstances that often seemed heroic to Samuel. This had not been the case for his father's side of the family. One of the consequences of this obvious difference between the two families was the splitting Samuel thereupon established: just as there were, for him, two kinds of vagina, two kinds of penis, etc., so there were two kinds of death—noble and shameful. That was also his reading of his father's fatal accident: on the one hand, a noble death, caused by the car accident, and on the other a shameful one, because he had drowned as a result of the accident.

It then became possible to work on integrating "emptiness" and "running away"—now that those issues could be seen to be meaningful, they could have at least a tentative representation. Hence the deferred awareness of the traumatic impact his father's death had had on Samuel: he had been thrown headlong into the engulfing void of a vagina-valley, in which he drowned because, in spite of the safety-belt/truss, he had not managed to stay afloat on the waves.

It also became obvious that Samuel's whole attitude with respect to castration—and his behaving as though he were castrated—allowed him to run away from his feelings of aggressiveness and hate, for in making him think immediately of the Shoah, they forced him to identify with the torturers.

The exciting mother

Behind this figure of the father and the trauma of his death, there lurked the shadow of an exciting—and therefore traumatizing—mother.

A series of very exciting erotic dreams illustrated this point. Most of the time his mother had a seductive attitude towards him and he would wake up after a wet dream. That made him think of his childhood enuresis and of his fear of regression. These dreams took him back to his childhood, when he was a young boy sharing a bedroom with his sister; thinking of her also aroused in him seduction fantasies. One day the question suddenly emerged: before he was four years old, where did he sleep? In his parents' bedroom? He had no memory of this at all. He decided to ask his mother; when he did, he discovered that she could not remember either. They then asked the person who was in service with them at the time. This woman reminded Samuel's mother that he did in fact sleep in his parents' bedroom until he was four. Why had his mother "forgotten"? "It's obviously the same for her as for me," he exclaimed, "a black hole!"

Around this time he met a young woman who was to take pride of place in his life and in his analysis. He had another dream, but made no association to it. He was making love to this young woman. Almost imperceptibly, she turned into a woman with his mother's features, dressed in a black dress, her face very pale and her lips the colour of blood. Once again he tried to get me to give him a reassuring answer to the questions he was asking himself: "I'm waiting for you to give me the answer to all my problems!"

Then, without warning, Samuel missed a whole fortnight's sessions. When he returned, he told me he had lived alone in a house in the country that had been lent to him. He had had several undeniable successes in both his private and professional life. He even included his "clinical cure"—he had just spent the night with his partner and had made love to her without being in the least bothered by his "symptom"!

After enumerating these successes—he was in fact quite surprised by them—he told me he did not know what else to say. This "hiatus" that paralysed him enabled me to link the "abandonment" he had made me feel to the "maternal abandonment" he himself had experienced recently when he discovered that his mother had no memories of what his earliest years had been like.

Samuel fell silent for some time, then thought of how his excitation remained constant; he found this "strange". Not only his own, but also the excitement he tried to arouse in other people. It represented his "struggle against being abandoned and feeling depressed," he told me. "But getting excited, for me, is mostly about trying to excite the other person. Once that person is 'hooked', I drop the whole thing!" "So that the other person goes on thinking about you?" I suggested. "In order to produce in other people what I recently discovered I had apparently been unable to bring about in my own mother," he added.

In the following session, he again thought about the woman dressed in black, the vamp/vampire in the dream in which the woman he was making love to gradually came to resemble his mother. The woman in black was obviously a woman in mourning. He had never thought of that. In fact he was unable to think about his mother's various "widowings". He used the term "widowings" to refer to the many family deaths she had encountered in her life: the orphan of parents who had died in a concentration camp, she was still a young woman when her husband died, and she had lost her younger sister shortly before. Samuel had never been able to tell me about that before in case he would drown in his own tears . . . as, in the past, in his urine.

From that point on, a whole portion of the traumatic events of his childhood could be addressed. The fulcrum was the mother-in-mourning beside the over-exciting mother with her disruptive potential. The coexistence in a single object of excitation relating to mourning and that relating to maternal deprivation set up within Samuel a kind of confusion that prevented him from identifying the source of each of these. That confusion had later tried to acquire some form of representation through his identificatory problems, the symptomatic expression of which was illustrated by, among other factors, his fetishism. It then became possible to understand the combined action of red (excitation) and black (mourning) in a vamp/vampire mother, with associations to red curtains, blood-stained *muletas* and *corridas* . . . that he had dreamt of in his first sessions when the transference space was just starting to be built up.

Excitation and eroticization

The difficulties encountered in the course of Samuel's analysis are a good illustration of certain deficiencies in the way his mind worked, in particular on the economic level. When we are confronted with this kind of psychological mind-set, the main feeling we have is that the patient was unable at the appropriate time to install a structuring auto-eroticism, one that has depth and modulation, in accordance with the equilibrium established between certain early cathexes.

This is one of the reasons for the fact that patients like Samuel find themselves in great difficulty as soon as some kind of relationship is set up. A whole fantasy universe is produced, focusing on action—and, indeed, in reality actions are never far behind.

Such patients find it difficult to contain certain representations that are not available for the mind to process (perhaps they do not even exist as representations); they tend to "run away" from psychic conflict, the excess of excitation and the resultant pain, and act them out. Painful affects are not so much repressed or counter-cathected as ejected outside of the mind and transformed into enactment (McDougall, 1982). The impossibility of integrating or deferring excitation in order to make it acceptable to the mind—by organizing, for example, an appropriate kind of masochism as a watchman over their lives (Rosenberg, 1982)—is also an important element in these personalities which, more often than not, tend towards perversion. Consequently, Samuel's transvestism could be understood as a fetishist solution to the anxiety aroused by his destructive and castration fantasies, with the resultant need to deny both of these.

Samuel's perverse scenarios could also be read as unfinished attempts to reach a goal, that of "curing" his premature ejaculation. In other words, the diagnosis in this case would be a failure of fetishism—the failure being in part due to an obstacle that prevented Samuel from utilizing denial of castration. In this sense, the frantic eroticization of a castration fantasy, emphasized throughout the analysis, would lend support to this hypothesis.

Samuel appeared never to have managed to acquire once and for all the capacity to differentiate between his erotogenic zones and the rest of his body. The excitable erotogenic zones were not contained within his representations of male and female genitalia. His mind-set was bound to collapse as soon as eroticism appeared on the scene, given that, for Samuel, eroticism involved only bodily sensations. Hence his genuine difficulty in processing and integrating the idea of "excitation" as compared to that of "no excitation". The power of his auto-eroticism blocked any possibility he had of mentalization and integration. His mental development seemed to have gone directly—without any Preconscious working-through—from enuresis to premature ejaculation. The result most of the time was that the mere contact with "wetness" in sexual intercourse implied, for Samuel, both pleasure and anxiety.

Samuel's transvestism was therefore a consequence of his inability to contrast or even to differentiate between his body as aroused by his desired object and the excitation that the object produced in him. His regression, when confronted with the Oedipal situation, made it clear that narcissistic problems were at the root of his condition. As a result, he could not set up an appropriate kind of auto-eroticism, at least as regards the point where auto-eroticism originates—the moment, always renewed, when sexuality becomes detached from the object of need and begins to generate fantasies, thereby establishing itself *qua* sexuality. This is also the point at which we see the first tentative signs of internalization of relationships linked to the object, thus heralding the possibility of mourning the loss of the illusion that the desired object will always be present to provide completeness—and this also has constantly to be renewed afresh.

When this process breaks down, auto-eroticism based on the significance attributed to the self's own body can set in, since it gives pride of place to narcissistic cathexes, in particular those that refer essentially to the body. The auto-erotic drive, as Green points out, is capable of satisfying itself, whether the object is absent or present, but in any case independently of it (Green, 1983). Auto-eroticism therefore belongs to that group of phenomena in which the body takes the place of the outside world.

For auto-erotic drives to function, they require the operation of maternal narcissistic cathexes, and the care the mother gives as she looks after her infant makes its own contribution, "covering", as it were, her infant's auto-eroticism. If there is no or very little cathexis derived from primary maternal narcissism, say Braunschweig and

Fain (1971), the erotogenic zone is excited—but to no avail, since there are no narcissistic resources available to focus on it. They suggest that something happened to premature ejaculators in the past that prevents their primary eroticism in the first place from keeping hold of a representation of the absent object, and, in the second, from taking pleasure in holding on to it. Since their sexual development has remained fixated at a primitive level of satisfaction that forces them to restrain sexual tension to a non-disruptive mode, via very brief physical contact with the object, it is therefore always short-circuited. Hence we could say that, in Samuel's case, the symptom functioned with two simultaneous deficiencies: there was hardly any restraint as regards active discharge, and no possibility of representing the absent object. He was completely unable to hold back acted-out discharge by means of represented discharge, or to take pleasure in holding on to representations; this activity in itself constitutes one form of auto-eroticism that is transformed into the pleasure of waiting for pleasure.

In short, the economic imbalance between body cathexes and excitation of erotogenic zones always has some repercussions. Samuel, for example, was unable to control those orifices he experienced as deprived of autonomous functioning, given that the auto-erotic pleasure associated with them was in conflict with an anaclitic object the loss of which was impossible to mourn. He was therefore obliged to set up a split-off and fetishist auto-eroticism based on body organs.

The work of the psychoanalyst

At certain moments in the analysis, Samuel gave me the impression of being a perfect—perhaps even macroscopic—illustration of what Freud wrote in his description of auto-eroticism:

> The characteristics of infantile sexual life which we have hitherto emphasized are the facts that it is essentially auto-erotic (i.e. that it finds its object in the infant's own body) and that its individual component instincts are upon the whole disconnected and independent of one another in their search for pleasure. [Freud, 1905d, p. 197]

Samuel's auto-eroticism brought about discharges of pleasure that to all intents and purposes were orgasms. Hence the organ-pleasure could change into "being mad for an orgasm". The manner in which the auto-erotic orgasm was displayed and thought about meant that it was not a substitute for verbal expression; it was there on its own behalf, as it were, as a supply of pure pleasure and sexual ecstasy—though there was perhaps more than a hint of genuine deep-rooted anxiety, the pregenital or even archaic origins of which were beyond doubt.

Paradoxically, at moments like those in the analysis, Samuel looked for support from the setting and from the analyst's presence; as a result, he was able to use these as props for resolving to some extent the drive-determined and psychic tension he experienced. They gave Samuel pleasure of the kind he apparently had never known before, a pleasure that he was determined to keep on discovering and rediscovering; the main driving forces behind this were excitation and sexual ecstasy. When they occurred in the sessions, they quite literally and directly became erotic enactments, short-circuiting the very notion of the psychoanalytic process. They bore witness to the counter-depressive struggle in which Samuel was engaged, a struggle that seemed all the more desperate and tragic because it was essentially related to Samuel's apparent incapacity to cathect a continuous object, thereby revealing his inability to set himself up as a depressive object. His thirst for excitation was therefore simply an anti-depressive defence.

Under such conditions—at one point or another they lead up to the question: is analysis possible with patients like Samuel?—the main task of the psychoanalyst consists in not being "engulfed" (going down with the *Titanic*) in and by the whirlwind of allo- or auto-erotic representations that block all possibility of following the trace(s) of the fantasy object (both conscious and unconscious).

Faced with such situations, psychoanalysts—for their own mental survival as well as for that of their patients—have to modulate and contain these excessive degrees of excitation. This offers the opportunity of building up mental representations, via constant linking and re-linking, that to start with were non-existent (because impossible to create). It is only after a great deal of prolonged and hard work that these representations can be cathected. Then they will be able to act as a protective shield—the protective barrier against excitation that had been lacking up till then. In other words, the work of counter-cathexis, exhausting for both patient and analyst, has to be transformed into something that, through linking, un-linking and re-linking, gives the mind an opportunity to create representations that can be cathected. Under these conditions, such representations become capable of making links and providing structure (Cournut, 1991).

Given that these patients are often in great difficulty whenever relationships are involved, the mental work required by the analyst is often extremely complex. When patients feel over-exposed to the test of the transference (and to the emotions the transference arouses in them), what emerges is the excitation derived from their difficulty in organizing and containing auto-eroticism, together with the sexual ecstasy that they gain from it. Then they attack the setting and the transference in order not to feel too dependent or constrained by them; the danger then is that they may jeopardize the continuity of the very cathexes they had originally come into analysis to look for.

Notes

1. See the *Revue Française de Psychanalyse*, *58*, 3 / 1993 for a discussion of "The child within the adult" (in French), and in particular the articles by R. Diatkine "L'enfant dans l'adulte ou l'éternelle capacité de reverie" (pp. 641–648) and F. Guignard "L'enfant dans le psychanalyste" (pp. 649–659).
2. [Translator's note: The French expression for "curled up like a foetus"—*chien de fusil*—also means "the hammer of a rifle".]

CHAPTER FIVE

The sexual sphere and the work of the analysis

I The Devil religion

Freud freely admitted that, though he felt considerable admiration for the great Russian writer Fiodor Dostoevsky, he did not care much for his personality. In a letter to Theodor Reik dated 14 April 1929, Freud wrote:

> You are right, too, in suspecting that, in spite of all my admiration for Dostoevsky's intensity and pre-eminence, I do not really like him. That is because my patience with pathological natures is exhausted in analysis. In art and life I am intolerant of them. Those are character traits personal to me and not binding on others. [Reik, 1940, quoted in Freud, 1928b, p. 196]

In his paper on Dostoevsky and parricide, Freud (1928b) stresses the fact that Dostoevsky was "[a] neurotic, [a] moralist and [a] sinner" (*ibid.*, p. 177). For Freud, these three epithets were enough to summarize the whole personality of the Russian writer; he used them to paint an extraordinary psychological portrait of Dostoevsky that brought together the latter's epilepsy (with the hypothesis that it was hysterical in origin), his moral masochism, and his strong bisexual tendencies (latent homosexuality and the negative form of the Oedipus complex) in an attempt to explore and to analyse the theme of parricide:

> He dealt first with the common criminal (whose motives are egotistical), and the political and religious criminal; and not until the end of his life did he come back to the primal criminal, the parricide, and use him, in a work of art, for making his confession. [*ibid.*, p. 190]

The central theme of this remarkable paper is essentially concerned with the analysis of the writer's unconscious guilt feelings. Linked to his unconscious death wishes concerning his father (who seems to have been particularly harsh, violent, and cruel) and reinforced by his masochistic behaviour (development of a superego that was sadistic towards a submissive, feminine, and passive ego), Dostoevsky's guilt feelings appeared to find some relief in his epileptic seizures—experienced in fact as punishments because of the writer's "father-identification on the part of his ego, which is permitted by his superego as a punishment" (*ibid.*, p. 185)

Dostoevsky between Freud and Reik

The year following its publication, this paper was severely criticized by Theodor Reik (Bokanowski, 1981). Though he agreed completely with Freud's psychoanalytic thesis—"[. . .] he masterfully opens the hidden way to the psyche" (Reik, 1940, p. 167)—Reik criticized Freud for writing an occasional piece that seemed to him to be much too moralistic as regards the great Russian writer and failed, in his view, to do justice to Dostoevsky's creative talent and capacity for sublimation: "[. . .] why does Freud's discussion of the concept of morality strike us as dubious and inadequate?" writes Reik (*ibid.*, p. 160), adding: "Should he not have given recognition to another aspect, that of the great psychologist?" (*ibid.*, p. 172).

Reik's criticism becomes even more subtle when he questions the fact that, in attempting to analyse Dostoevsky's passion for gambling ("*le jeu pour le jeu*"), Freud bases his approach on Stefan Zweig's short story "Four-and-twenty hours in a woman's life". Reik again:

> It seems strange that Freud, usually so good at ordering his material economically, should devote four pages out of a twenty-six-page study of Dostoevsky—nearly one-sixth, that is—to a parenthetical illustration. With all due respect to Zweig's literary merit, we cannot help feeling that this is an error in proportion. It is as though a medieval artist painting the Passion of Christ should place in the foreground of the picture the bishop of his native diocese. [*ibid.*]

Freud's reading of Zweig's short story led him to suggest that the Russian writer's obsession with gambling[1] could be explained by his fixation with onanism. In the novella, a woman suddenly falls passionately in love with a man young enough to be her son who suffers from a destructive passion for gambling. In an attempt to break the habit in the young man, she seduces him and offers him her love . . . but in vain, because it does not prevent her young lover from being drawn back to gambling and, later, from putting a tragic end to his life by committing suicide.

Freud did accept that some of Reik's criticisms were well-founded. In the above-mentioned letter to Reik, he writes:

> I cannot dispute the unharmonious effect produced by the addition of the Zweig analysis; [. . .] If I had not been hampered by considerations of the place where my essay was to appear, I should certainly have written: "We may expect that in the history of a neurosis accompanied by such a severe sense of guilt a special part will be played by the struggle against masturbation. This expectation is completely fulfilled by Dostoevsky's pathological addiction to gambling. For, as we can see from a short story of Zweig's . . . etc." [. . .] All the same, the outcome was clumsy. [Reik, 1940, quoted in Freud, 1928b, pp. 195–196]

We could therefore interpret this apparently discordant impression that Freud himself called clumsy as the sign of a symptom concerning Dostoevsky and his writings. What could have compelled Freud to comment on a story involving a woman so charmed by a man young enough to be her son that she seduced him, especially since, as he finally admitted, there was no real need to do so given the main thesis of his paper? In other words, what reasons might have led Freud to shift from parricide and a son's death wish with respect to his father to the theme of seduction—

and, more specifically, that of a son being seduced by a mother figure?[2]

We may recall that at the beginning of his 1928 paper, Freud insists on Dostoevsky's *criminal tendencies*; in his novels, the Russian writer gave priority to "violent, murderous and egoistic characters" (Freud 1928b, p. 178), perhaps related to "the existence of similar tendencies within himself and also (to) certain facts in his life, like his passion for gambling and his possible confession to a sexual assault upon a young girl" (*ibid.*). It would seem, therefore, that in Freud's thinking and writing, Dostoevsky's passion for gambling and his paedophile tendencies were very closely related. In attempting to avoid mentioning a father's paedophile tendencies with respect to his (male or female) child, Freud displaced this theme in his paper on to a seductive and incestuous maternal figure—who at that point becomes much more noble than a paedophile father, given that the maternal seduction has as its ultimate aim the protection of the seduced child from his or her auto-erotic excitement and feelings![3]

Thanks, apparently, to this displacement, Freud's study of Dostoevsky was able to avoid the thorny question of the father's Eros and, even more, the consequences (especially on his status as father) of his unbridled sensuality . . . It seems reasonable to suppose that what Freud disliked in Dostoevsky—and in particular in *The Brothers Karamazov*—was the way the writer used paternal sensuality and the (sensual and perverse) passion it creates to the detriment of paternity, filiation and the status of both.[4]

This may make sense of another similar displacement that, in spite of its oddity, does not appear until now to have inspired any particular comments from those who have studied the text. In his comparison of *The Brothers Karamazov* with *Oedipus Rex* and with *Hamlet*, Freud (1928b, pp. 188–189) makes this surprising statement with respect to the Greek tragedy:

> The hero (Oedipus) commits the deed unintentionally and apparently uninfluenced by the woman; this latter element is however taken into account in the circumstance that the hero can only obtain possession of the queen mother after he has repeated his deed upon the monster who symbolizes the father. [*ibid.*, p. 188]

It would seem, once again, that the issue of paternal sensuality and the father's feminine seductiveness, awakened by Dostoevsky's hero, led Freud to transform the monster—in other words, the Sphinx, a female figure—into a representation of the father. Perhaps he was driven to see in the Sphinx a reflection of Laïos: behind the paternal imago lurked a monstrous feminine double that was seductive and paedophile.[5]

"Unfortunately, my own father . . ."

We could, therefore, suggest that, when Freud found himself confronted with Dostoevsky's personality and the sensual and instinctual qualities of the writer's heroic figures, he felt indirectly propelled back to an era that, to him, smacked of heresy, an era he still had to push into the background—the years between 1895 and 1897, when he was working on his *neurotica*.

Freud spent those two years, while he was working on his seduction theory, demonstrating that the etiological roots of hysteria could well lie in the fact that a child who did not yet have any real possibility of understanding what was going on had been sexually seduced by a perverted adult. He thought at that time he could establish a link between sexuality, trauma, and pathological defences. This period, during which the seduction theory flared up then died down, was a convulsive episode rooted in Freud's passionate nature (Gantheret, 1988), which fed on his transference relationship with Fliess, later acknowledged as unconsciously homosexual.

Freud abandoned his *neurotica*—his "I no longer believe in my *neurotica*" dates from 21 September 1897 (Freud, 1950a, p. 259)—after his self-analysis, one year after his father Jacob died in October 1896. That same year, as he was working through the necessary mourning process for his father, Freud drew up a series of hypotheses in the space of just a few weeks:

- Fathers (or uncles) are the instigators of seduction (Letter to Fliess, January 11, 1897);
- Hysteria is the negative of perversion.

> If only I knew why the Devil's semen is always described as 'cold' in the witches' confessions! I have ordered a copy of *Malleus*

> *Maleficarum* and [. . .] I shall study it diligently. [. . .] I have an idea shaping in my mind that in the perversions, of which hysteria is the negative, we may have before us a residue of a primaeval sexual cult which, in the Semitic east (Moloch, Astarte), was once, perhaps still is a religion.
>
> Perverse actions, moreover, are always the same—with a meaning and made on some pattern which it will be possible to understand.
>
> I dream, therefore, of a primaeval Devil religion, whose rites are carried on secretly, and I understand the severe therapy of the witches' judges. [Letter to Fliess, 24 January 1897; Freud, 1950a, p. 243).

- Finally, there came the idea that even his own father may, after so many seducing fathers, have been a frightening or even diabolical figure because of his seductiveness and perversion:

> Unfortunately, my own father was one of these perverts and is responsible for the hysteria of my brother (all of whose symptoms are identifications) and those of several younger sisters. The frequency of this circumstance often makes me wonder. [Letter to Fliess, 8 & 11 February 1897, quoted in Masson, 1985, pp. 230–231]

Thus, Freud put aside his *neurotica* in September 1897 after the emergence—somewhat prematurely, it would seem, since he would quickly abandon the idea—of issues involving the passive homosexual wishes this paternal figure implies. But it was not until *Leonardo da Vinci and a Memory of his Childhood* (1910c) and the case study of Senatspräsident Schreber (1911c) that Freud was able to theorize the underlying passive homosexual tendency he feared—at that particular point in his psychoanalytic development (January–February 1897)—to see emerge in the figure of Jacob Freud. It was much later, in his paper on *The Ego and the Id* (1923b) that he worked out a theoretical formulation of the negative form of the Oedipus complex. We could suggest that this underlying passive homosexual tendency with respect to the paternal figure, after the demise of Jacob Freud, returned to the foreground and awakened Sigmund Freud's interest in the *Malleus Maleficarum* and the *Devil religion*, whose obscene and terrifying cult led him, as he wrote, to *dream* . . .

In abandoning his *neurotica*, Freud could no longer maintain that trauma was necessarily based on an historical event the functional character of which served as a foundation for traumatic reality: henceforth, the road was open for the discovery of a new space, that of intrapsychic reality in which the criteria of ordinary reality do not apply. However, the true soil of fantasy—including the fantasy of seduction—continued to run through all of Freud's thinking, for he never entirely abandoned his original model: "I have gone beyond that theory, but I have not abandoned it; that is to say, I do not today consider the theory incorrect, but incomplete" (Freud, 1905e, n. 27). The uncompromising force of clinical evidence maintained a state of "tension" between fantasy and the soil in which fantasy takes root. This led Freud in the years that followed to suggest that, in human beings, sexuality is essentially and fundamentally traumatic; he was then able to put forward the concept of *primal fantasies* as organizers of the human mind.

This meant that he had to explore the idea of seduction much more thoroughly. He did this by operating a radical reversal of his initial assumptions to take into account a twofold change in the original structure:

- the psychopathological model of seduction was no longer the paedophile and incestuous father–daughter or father–son seduction, but the fantasy of incestuous desires between son and mother (and, later, passive homosexual desires between son and father);
- the crucial element in the new model was no longer the father's erotic complex with respect to his male or female offspring, but the son's (or even daughter's) similarly incestuous attachment to the mother;
- put generally, in abandoning his *neurotica*, Freud's purpose was to abandon the adult's erotic complex with respect to a child in favour of the child's with respect to an adult.

Henceforth, as in his analysis of the Wolf-Man (Freud, 1918b)—exemplary from this point of view—Freud tried every time he could to discover the real event, while maintaining the analysis suspended and immersed in intrapsychic reality. In the Wolf-Man, traumatic reality derived from his witnessing the primal scene, but it was the dream that constituted the real trauma: reality and fantasy are closely connected in the structure of seduction theory.

From the child's innocent "tenderness" to the adult's perverse "passionate" language

It is, therefore, quite possible to understand the deep-rooted reasons that prevented Freud, haunted as he was by the fear of some new theoretical deviation modelled on the pattern of the *neurotica*, from seeing the genuine epistemological leap proposed by Ferenczi in Vienna, when he gave Freud a preview of the lecture he had prepared for the XIIth International Congress of Psychoanalysis in Wiesbaden in September 1932; this paper was later published under the title "Confusion of tongues between adults and the child. The language of tenderness and of passion" (Ferenczi, 1949). We know that Freud's reaction on reading this paper was quite unpleasant.

Freud blamed Ferenczi for introducing new techniques (relaxation and neo-catharsis), and feared they would lead him into paths far removed from the orthodox one. His main dread was that, with his new theoretical proposals, Ferenczi might be tempted to defend the fact that he was taking liberties with orthodox technique.

Ferenczi's hypotheses principally concerned a new metapsychological formulation of seduction theory in relation to the theory of trauma—he argued the case for the inevitability of actual seduction. Today there is no doubt that Ferenczi's contributions to thinking about the nature of trauma and extending the meaning of the term—in particular to include a narcissistic dimension—enabled a decisive step forward to be made.

Ferenczi started from the difficulties and unsatisfactory results (and sometimes outright failures) he met with in treating certain adult patients. He felt that one of the main reasons for this was that the analyst did not take enough account of the reality of certain trauma suffered in the past by these patients.

> A typical way in which incestuous seductions may occur is this: an adult and a child love each other, the child nursing the playful phantasy of taking the rôle of mother to the adult. This play may assume erotic forms but remains, nevertheless, on the level of tenderness. It is not so, however, with pathological adults [. . .] They mistake the play of children for the desires of a sexually mature person or even allow themselves—irrespective of any consequences—to be carried away. [Ferenczi, 1949, p. 227]

Contrasting "the tenderness of the infantile eroticism (with) the passionate in the sexuality of the adult", Ferenczi (*ibid.*, p. 230) went on to describe how the child (patient), excited and helpless, overwhelmed by too much excitation (external and, above all, internal) and without the means at his or her disposal either for discharge or for integration, is thereby placed in an extremely distressing situation. This picture enabled Ferenczi to put forward certain concepts such as *identification with the aggressor* and *introjection* by the child of the adult's *guilt feelings*—thereby increasing the confusion of feelings both in the child's internal world and in reality, and making for a true narcissistic splitting. To the passionate love and impassioned punishment inflicted by the adult is added the terrorism of suffering, in other words the obligation imposed on the child to look after, repair and care for a damaged parent. In this way passionate states and passionate transference develop.

Freud, followed by several analysts of the time, was apparently unable to appreciate the true value of Ferenczi's basic theoretical hypothesis: that seduction is experienced as an *introjective identification* (what is introjected is then subjected to the principle of primary mental functioning and transformed into hallucination and hallucinated memory). All they seemed able to grasp was the danger of theoretical regression. Fearing the abandonment of the idea that, in children, trauma, like narcissistic wounds, is the result of the emergence of fantasy organization, Freud could see in Ferenczi's innovative hypotheses only a return to the seduction theory. This theory, with its inherent risk that the imago of a seductive, paedophile and perverse father figure might re-appear, meant that certain questions involving the father's Eros (seduction, homophilia, homosexuality, paedophilia, etc.) would have to be addressed, together with the impact of the paternal Eros on the psychopathological structure of certain individuals.

From the father's Eros to the erotic father

The father's Eros and sensuality, to describe which the term "erotic father" seems appropriate, is a "construct that associates two essentially conflicting terms," writes Michel Fain, adding:

> The idea of the father which, according to Freud, is posterior to the totemistic regime that followed the tyrant's murder by the primal

> horde, lays claim to a kind of legitimacy derived from totemistic taboos. This legitimacy gives a degree of power that the tyrant of the primal horde never had while he was alive, power which remains tied to a representation of the father as lacking in sexual desire. To describe the father as "erotic" runs counter to the very events that led to the concept of fatherhood. [Fain, 1987, p. 20]

The essential implication of fatherhood is that the father—in his multiple role as prohibiting, reassuring and tender—protects the child from his or her own incestuous desires and helps transform them into a well-modulated auto-eroticism. This kind of protection operates under the guise of prohibition, and constitutes the phallic aspect of the father (his male member, as it were)[6] that enables the mother not to fall asleep in the incestuous slumber of her child. Similarly, in protecting his son or daughter's id from any insufficiently-modulated auto-erotic instinctuality of his own, the father protects his offspring from the consequences of the extreme psychic violence he would otherwise inflict on them (because of the inexhaustible sources of excitation his unbridled id would represent).

If the paternal erotic grammar (excessive sensuality, paedophilia, homosexuality that is not simply latent and integrated in the mind, etc.) is too obvious or too excessive, it imprints a significant degree of sexualization on the ego instincts of the child. Hence, the possibility of a traumatic eroticization of sado-masochistic positions with respect to the kind of father who, through excessive sexuality and sexualization, maintains a permanent (and therefore violent) state of excitability.

The father's paedophilia—the extreme form of his homosexuality—derives from his rejection and hatred of auto-erotic sexuality, both in himself and in his child. His violence is expressed as a narcissistic hatred of his child's sexual drive, related to the fantasy wound that his (male or female) child's unconscious sexuality entails. In fact, when this hatred becomes too strong and is confronted with the violence it engenders, it changes into seduction-complicity and promiscuity. This is the point at which incestuous attempts originate.

Focused on his own narcissism, the father cannot accept that harm be done to his narcissistic ideals. He has then to transform his child into a narcissistic "double" whose role, in a fantasy of sexual promiscuity, is to compensate for the failure of the links that would have enabled him to set up a well-modulated homosexuality. Given the failure of the processes whereby primary homosexuality can shift towards latent and psychic secondary homosexuality, homosexuality can only be acted out or expressed in a regressive manner.

In other words, this kind of father experiences a highly conflicting situation with respect to passive homosexual desires, given the violent contrast between homosexual and narcissistic aspects. Such men are sometimes impelled to act out their eroticism with children (as doubles of themselves) because of the insufficient infrastructure of the primary homosexual relationship in regard to the mother who, in the past, was too adhesively attached (in fantasy) to the son, too seductive and intrusive—and therefore traumatic.

Subjected to randomly excessive stimulation in their early interactions with the object—or, conversely, to a complete lack of stimulation—these fathers develop compensatory auto-eroticism that is unsatisfying in so far as it does not grow out of links with the object but takes over the object's place (or, sometimes, sits in opposition to it). When they seek out excitement and try to compensate for the excessive or missing stimulation contributed by the object, they sometimes give in to incestuous violence that in fact derives from their hatred of anything sexual or auto-erotic.

What usually appears in analysis is how the indirect effects of the destiny of paedophile impulses operate—due to repression, for example, or suppression. This was the case with Gilles. In the years following the birth of his sons, he suffered from impulses to "strangle" them. These made him feel very anxious and guilt-ridden, and were indeed part of the reasons that brought him to analysis. During his treatment, the transference situation enabled us to clarify and to elucidate this symptom; we discovered that it was linked to massive repression of his psychic homosexuality in relation to his paedophilic desires. His father had been violent towards him as a child, and Gilles had lived in fear of him throughout his boyhood. The family had formerly lived in a vast domain and had kept many servants, including a male cook towards whom Gilles had felt particularly attracted. The psychoanalytic situation brought back into his mind memories of the happiness he had felt when, after some particularly violent scene or other with his father, he would rush to the chef and find comfort in his embrace. Given that Gilles' transference contained a strong homosexual element, we were able to do quite significant work on de-condensation and re-establishing links with respect to representations of his impulses: these were related to his fear of wanting to be "held" and to "hold himself" in a man's arms—his father's, the chef's and, through them, mine; this led him to create sodomy-type fantasies he experienced as shameful.

From time to time in certain psychopathological patterns we see the secondary (and belated) effects of the father's acts of paedophilia with respect to his son. This was the case with Gauthier, who had asked for psychotherapeutic help because of major problems concerning his personality and self-identity. As a child, his father had subjected him to various procedures that were intended to seduce him—he regularly verified the cleanliness of Gauthier's anus and repeatedly made him have enemas. The boy experienced these as deeply distressing intrusions, and at the same time felt very ashamed. Thanks to the work we did together in the therapy, these memories, together with others even more deeply buried, were recalled and gave rise to the idea that his father's perverse manoeuvres had none the less sometimes given him some degree of pleasure. This distressed him considerably and, though he claimed to be grateful for the work we had accomplished, he decided to put an end to the therapy. I later learned that from time to time—and on each occasion with a great deal of ambiguity—he would consult other analysts in order to "verify" that no one would try to be as "penetrating" with him as his father had been in the past—and as I, too, unwittingly, had given him the impression of being in our sessions.

A diabolical father

As is clear from Senatspräsident Schreber's *Memoirs*, it is possible to suffer from the absence of a "legally" constructed castration complex. Faced with this, the only recourse he had was to construct a delusion, the main theme of which was built around the delight he took in imagining the designs of father–God who desired him and made him believe "that after all it really must be very nice to be a woman submitting to the act of copulation" (Freud, 1911c, p. 20).

The same was perhaps true of the seventeenth-century painter Christopher Haitzmann. He suffered from a "demonological neurosis" (Freud, 1923d), and his "apparitions of the Devil"—attempts to cure his "melancholia"—made Freud think that Haitzmann's representation of the devil was taken from the relationship of fear, hate and deep ambivalence that he may have experienced with respect to his father.

In proposing to interpret the figure of the devil as a paternal substitute, Freud tried to take into account the kind of relationship that, for the artist, persecution by the devil evoked (bonds, possession, apparitions). Taking as his starting point reproductions of some of Haitzmann's paintings, together with the painter's Diary (written between September 1677 and January 1678)—included in the 'Trophy of Mariazell'—Freud was particularly attentive to certain clues, especially those relating to the *feminine* characteristics of the devil as he appeared to the painter at that time. Freud claimed that the presence of these characteristics was in contradiction to the hypothesis of the devil as a paternal substitute; he added that this way of representing the devil was "unusual":

> This stressing of the female sexual character by introducing large pendulous breasts (there is never any indication of the female genitals) is bound to appear to us as a striking contradiction of our hypothesis that the Devil has the meaning of a father-substitute for the painter. And, indeed, such a way of representing the Devil is in itself unusual [. . .] That *the* Devil, who is a great individuality, the Lord of Hell and the Adversary of God, should be represented otherwise than as a male, and, indeed, as a super-male, with horns, tail and a big penis-snake—this, I believe, is never found. [Freud 1923d, pp. 89–90]

A little further on, Freud writes: "But why should his father, after being reduced to the status of a Devil, bear this physical mark of a woman?"

Starting from these female elements appended to the devil by Haitzmann in his paintings, Freud proposes a certain number of interpretations:

- the painter's revolt against his own feminine position which created fantasies of being pregnant (related to mourning and nostalgia after the death of his father);

- the ensuing struggle against castration anxiety, leading Haitzmann to project his femininity (i.e., his passive and feminine state of mind) on to the Father–Devil figure;
- and, finally, displacement on to the father figure of the painter's own infantile tenderness derived from his past relationship with his mother.

These interpretations all seek to shed light on the episodes of possession by the devil in Christopher Haitzmann's illness, and they highlight the relationship and mental links between father and son. They do, however, appear to ignore one significant aspect of the relationship between the painter and the devil which focuses on the idea of possession and being possessed by the devil, thereby belonging to him *body and soul*, as is indicated in the second bond with Satan.[7] In his analysis, as well as in drafting his paper, Freud seems to have ignored (and perhaps abandoned) the complex situation arising from the fact that the devil seduces the painter, even though seduction is very much an issue in Haitzmann's wish to feel possessed and to have his body "bounden" in this manner.

Freud gives the impression of pushing to one side any interpretation of the devil's female features as the artist's expression of a feminine father driven by seductive and incestuous desires with respect to his son. There would seem to be no place in Freud's thinking for a devil-father with female features that would perhaps have reminded him too closely of the time—still worrying, hellish and mephitic—when *neurotica* dominated his thoughts. This being so, Freud had to conceive of and idealize a purely male devil by refusing to grant him any female attributes—indeed by turning these into something invented by Haitzmann as an expression of the painter's own unconscious impulses concerning the relationship between father and son. In other words, for Freud, Haitzmann can love the devil-father only on condition that this figure has nothing feminine about it.[8]

But what exactly was Freud rejecting here? Apparently the very idea of some degree of femininity in the father as well as any possibility of seducing the son that could follow on from that. The "possessed–seduced" son, tied to his "declaration of love", gives himself over "body and soul" to the devil–father he loves. Here, obviously, the devil is the psychic representation of a father seducing his son, just as the son is a "possessed–seduced" figure who places himself in a passive and feminine position. The devil, with his female attributes, is attracted by the son's masculinity. The relationship between father and son then becomes one of homosexual seduction, behind which we can discern the imago of a phallic mother—or a representation of the combined parents, sexually united, fused one with the other, terrifying and (because of this) hated.

"Father, don't you see?"

Interpreting Haitzmann's instinctual urges with regard to the devil–father as an expression of the negative form of the painter's Oedipal desires meant that Freud could put aside the hypothesis that the sensual father, overwhelmed by his own impulses, had a desire to seduce. More than twenty-five years after abandoning his *neurotica*, the imago of the perverse seducing father threatened to remind Freud of certain old theoretical demons which, at that point, involved devilish fathers who perhaps spawned a hellish, obscene, and terrifying cult . . . going by the name of paedophilia.

In attempting to see in the devil only a father with absolutely no trace of femininity, Freud was probably trying to protect himself from painful memories related to the intense mourning process he had gone through in the year following the death of his father, Jacob. That mourning process was all the more distressing since it was so closely connected to the various theoretical upheavals Freud had had to confront, given the progress his self-analysis was making. By refusing to acknowledge the imago of a feminine father, Freud was perhaps also trying to avoid feeling trapped in an identification with the depression and mourning that Haitzmann was going through after the death of *his* father.

In his preface to the second edition of *The Interpretation of Dreams*, Freud stresses the fact that, after finishing the book, he felt it had been written in reaction to his father's death: "It was, I found, a portion of my own self-analysis, my reaction to my father's death—that is to say, to the most important event, the most poignant loss, of a man's life" (Freud, 1900a, p. xxvi).

It seems reasonable to suggest, therefore, that mourning for his father was followed by that for some latent representation of the father–son relationship, in particular involving the feverish, even burning, desire expressed in the incestuous seduction of a child by the father.

This may also shed light on the significance Freud attributes to the poignant dream known as "the burning child"; Freud commented on it in an epigraph to Chapter Seven of *The Interpretation of Dreams*.[9] The latent content of the dream indirectly confronts the reader with the burning desire of a father for his child . . . and with the latter's death. The dream represents a sympathetic excitation undoubtedly linked to sexuality, mourning, and guilt. The tone is tragic, and the words pronounced by the child—"Father, don't you see I'm burning?"—recall those of the boy in Goethe's poem *The Erl-King*:

> "My father, my father, and dost thou not see,
> How the Erl-King his daughters has brought here for me?"
> "My darling, my darling, I see it aright,
> 'Tis the aged grey willows deceiving thy sight."
> "I love thee, I'm charm'd by thy beauty, dear boy!
> And if thou'rt unwilling, then force I'll employ."
> "My father, my father, he seizes me fast,
> Full sorely the Erl-King has hurt me at last."
> The father now gallops, with terror half wild,
> He grasps in his arms the poor shuddering child;
> He reaches his courtyard with toil and with dread,—
> The child in his arms finds he motionless, dead.[10]

II Psychic homosexuality: the manifest content of which latent ones?[11]

As a component of the organization of psychic bisexuality in both sexes, psychic homosexuality is a concept that, according to its most common definition, ultimately denotes a specific state of mind in a person being analysed, a contextual mind-set that coincides with a precise movement, or even a precise moment, in the treatment. For many male and female psychoanalysts, it is an essential reference point in men, in whom it is traditionally described as constituting the structuring role of passive homosexuality in regard to the relationship with the father, while also reflecting the degree of repression of the analysand's passive–feminine component during the course of psychoanalytic treatment.

However, what does the term "psychic homosexuality" itself cover? Should it be seen as a synonym overlapping or interchangeable with the more frequently used concepts of unconscious homosexuality and latent homosexuality? What intersections of the bisexual organization of the analysand's psyche confront the psychoanalyst when he or she has occasion to refer to this concept? What uses may be made of it in the analyst's thought processes, both on a personal level (the analyst's own psychic homosexuality) and while treating a male or female patient?

What types of link exist between psychic homosexuality and the *homosexual motion of the instinct*, which is considered to be organized in both sexes around the "penis", in the form of an attachment to a phallic-narcissistic object? Does psychic homosexuality refer specifically to the male aspect, in the sense in which Freud said that libido is "of a masculine nature" (Freud, 1905d, p. 219)?

However, in invoking psychic homosexuality at all, are we not essentially talking about the *negative form of the Oedipal psychic organization* that is a normal and necessary component of bisexuality in both sexes, i.e., the so-called *structuring* psychic position whose economic basis is anality? What is the situation in women? Is psychic homosexuality to be deemed to cover the entire daughter–mother relationship, or is it confined to the organization of primary attachment? How should we then see certain movements of male identification aimed at seducing the mother? In other words, what are the links between psychic homosexuality and the primary relationship with the mother, secondary homosexuality and homosexuality that is acted out?

Since Freud added his famous note to the "Dora" analysis in 1923 ("Before I had learnt the importance of the homosexual current of feeling in psychoneurotics, I was often brought to a standstill in the treatment of my cases or found myself in complete perplexity" (Freud, 1905e, p. 120)), a very large number of important publications have been devoted to psychic homosexuality. These now provide us with a better grasp of some of the complexities of this concept, whose everyday use seems to us a matter of routine and whose handling is essential to all of us for the understanding of a certain type of material.

Two analyses (of a male and a female patient respectively) led me to formulate some questions on the possible implications of this concept.

When mother climbs up a ladder . . .

This vignette presents an important and defining moment of transformation in the psychoanalytic treatment of a patient whom I will call Julien. The moment was significant not only for the patient himself but also for my understanding of certain psychic modalities that he had evidenced since the beginning of his psychoanalysis. The analytic fragment to be examined here hinges on a transference dream of the homosexual erotic type.

> Lying naked on a bed with his male business partner, he asks the latter to "lick" his anus . . . The partner replies that he finds such practices disgusting . . ..

Julien hesitated for a long time before reporting this dream in the session. Owing to his—to say the least—scabrous situation in the dream, and the crude fantasy thereby betrayed, he found it very difficult to have to tell me about it. What made the need to report it even more painful was that he could not see why he should have had such a dream. The partner was a man younger than himself, with whom he got on well and whom he liked very much. Their professional relationship and friendship dated from approximately the same time as the beginning of Julien's analysis. This, together with other factors, tended to confirm the manifestly transference aspect of the dream. This movement also formed part of the context of transference repetition and elaboration of the infantile conflicts that had brought Julien into analysis.

He had consulted me after the birth of his third child, a third son: since he himself was the third child in a family of four, the birth of this son took him back to his own childhood and to various problems of identification associated with it, which he now wished to try to clear up. Of the four children, he was the best loved by his parents, who had separated during his teens when the mother could tolerate the father's "character" no longer. The father was depressive with a complex personality, liable to this day to a severe character disorder which made him "hateful" to everyone around him. Julien, who was deeply attached to his mother, told me that his childhood and adolescence had been characterized by *terrified submission* on his part to his father's mood swings, whereas his brothers and sisters had quickly been able to show their hostility and thereafter be apparently independent.

In the transference, Julien's analysis had been marked from the beginning by intense Oedipal guilt experienced in relation to his father. This had been reinforced by his father's manifest signs of affection towards him and by the need to repair the father's image, which contrasted in every respect with that of an idealizable and hitherto idealized mother. Julien had been remarkably successful in his professional career and had shown great financial generosity towards his family—so that he thus currently found himself playing a paternal role. The resulting sense of guilt had been exacerbated by his own fatherhood, which had become intolerable following the birth of this third son, identification with whom had reawakened all his Oedipal issues.

The immediate interpretation of this dream—to the effect that Julien was denouncing or even attacking his analyst by treating him as an *"arse-licker"*, just as he felt the other members of the family had formerly experienced him as his father's *"arse-licker"* (projective identification)—was therefore relatively obvious.

However, I decided for a number of reasons not to communicate this interpretation right away: apart from the fact that it might have reinforced a certain form of eroticization of the transference, it seemed to me at the time to carry the risk that Julien might experience it as a defensively homosexual interpretation on my part. Again, this dream had come during the course of a regressive movement that had begun a few sessions earlier, and I felt it important to allow that process to continue to develop more fully.

This regressive movement had started with an initial dream, which had awakened my attention and to some extent alerted me: "Julien is by the seaside, looking out over the ocean. Suddenly he sees a huge wave building up, a wave that will carry all before it . . . He is afraid it will swallow him up, together with his wife and children . . . He then tries to take shelter in a rickety-looking hut (*cabanon*), which he does not expect to stand up to the tidal wave . . .". Julien's associations to his dream were essentially indicative of a profound sense of panic and helplessness (in the true sense of Freud's Hilflosigkeit), coupled with the feeling of being at a complete loss and stunned ("pinned" to the spot). They immediately suggested to me that this dream was an attempt to represent in a metaphorical way an instinctual movement he had let slip, in the form of this immense breaker; it was a "non-integrated", "non-fused" instinctual movement "unmitigated by any protective shield against stimuli", which had arisen abruptly within him and could only assume a terrifying aspect at this point, so much so that it was like a breaker.[12] As I tried to imagine what this huge wave or "wall of water" that was about to crash down might represent, it seemed to me that perhaps it reflected some danger deriving from his Oedipal instincts. Projected on to me, they aroused terror in him. He was afraid that they could not be contained either by himself or by me, by virtue of the apparently worrying state of the *cabanon*, his protective shield against stimuli, which he was projecting on to me in the same movement.

Among Julien's associations in the session after this dream of the "breaker", he mentioned for the first time that his mother had had a miscarriage and an abortion. The miscarriage had occurred before his own birth, while the abortion had followed the birth of his younger brother. He remembered the abortion episode, because, he said, his mother had had to go abroad for the operation and had left the children alone with their father, asking them all to "manage as best they could", after filling the refrigerator with food to tide them over during her absence. In this session he came to ask himself whether these dead children might be present in himself: to what extent might these dead and voided children—especially the one lost in the miscarriage before his own birth—not have been himself? It followed that his mother, who had to his mind hitherto been "perfect"—he had "idealized" her throughout his childhood and adolescence and did so even now, as she seemed to him to be in sharp contrast in every respect to his father, on whom everything "bad" was projected—became less idealizable: for had she not deprived human beings of their lives (she had been an "abortionist", a "maker of angels")?

In a movement of anxiety that assailed him in relation to women, especially those close to him (his wife, his sister, his mother), he had occasion in the next session to mention a new aspect concerning his sister: she was "peculiar" (being of a mystical bent, she had apparently had several Zen Buddhist type experiences). He then recounted an anecdote which had at the time troubled him: his mother had recently told him of a "hallucinatory" kind of experience she had herself had in a cathedral while on a trip out of town. She had "climbed" the rungs of a ladder left standing against a column and had found herself at the very top holding a "hammer" in her hand (?) . . . After his comments on what he experienced as his sister's "fragility", this story increased Julien's concerns about his mother's mental health.

It did, however, cast new light on the "*rickety hut* (*cabanon*)" aspect of the "*breaker*" dream, introducing as it did madness and the padded cell in which disturbed lunatics are secluded.[13] It was now possible to interpret this dream as a representation of his transference anxiety, for which I suggested the following translation to him: "The anxiety and madness which the analysis arouses in you have turned into a huge breaker, and you do not know whether I, the 'analyst-as-rickety-hut (*cabanon*)', am solid and sane enough to be able to protect you from it . . ."

It was in the very next session after this one that Julien brought the dream of the business partner he asked to lick his anus.

Before telling me this dream, he had complained a great deal of having felt "impotent" with his wife, thinking that he no longer desired her. This had moreover revived a wish (which was painful to his ego ideal) to revert to sexual practices with prostitutes, in which he had indulged in the past, but which he wished to forget. Julien's adolescence and young adult life had been characterized by genuine sexual problems associated with intense "shyness", resulting from a sense that he lacked virility and from his difficulties over contact with women. For many years he had been able to have intercourse only with prostitutes.

As noted above, in order not to interfere with the integration process I felt to be imminent in the transference, I made a deliberate decision not to intervene at this point: in the context of the material of the preceding sessions, this dream seemed to me to belong to a psychic movement in which Julien was having recourse to a paternal third party, recourse which partially failed—holding on to an erotic homosexual transference indicates the very inadequacy of the attempt to obtain support from the father. This movement clearly demonstrates the conflictuality associated with Julien's wish to overcome his castration anxieties in relation to his mother who "climbed up the ladder" and his "peculiar" sister. His recourse to homosexuality proved insufficiently structuring: not only did it not allow him to emerge from his conflict, but in fact it plunged him straight back into it.

During this session I began to wonder about Julien's internal mother image: might it not possess the characteristics of a mother containing a dead, anal, and faecalized object (the miscarriage and the abortion)? Might this dead, faecalized object be for him partly responsible for his mother's inability to act as a container and help him fuse his instinctual drives? It seemed to me that the search for the instinctual fusion necessary for establishing links to his primary objects, both paternal and maternal, had brought about this crudely homosexual transference movement in him. It had brought him back to castration and to the "phallic/castrated" problem by way of submissiveness to the father, himself castrated, towards whom one could only act as an "arse-licker"; it also seemed to me to be connected with his castration anxieties as aroused by women, which were becoming condensed with the anxiety generated by a maternal imago containing a dead object.

Julien arrived very depressed for the next session, which followed a weekend break. He associated his depressive feelings with the fits of depression suffered by his father, who had in the past apparently even spoken of "suicidal ideas". I intervened to say, "Yes, but in an earlier session did you not tell me about something else as well . . .?" He then remembered having mentioned his mother's departure for the abortion, and this enabled him to find a link between the mention of this memory and his weekend depression.

On the following day, he brought another memory, which had come up in the meantime: his mother had once told him that, as a teenager during the war, she had been caught in an air raid in a provincial town. While running away amidst ruins and dead bodies strewn over the road, she had come upon a decapitated head. "Stunned", she could not prevent herself stopping to pick up the head, wrap it in a cloth (like a dead child?) and try to find someone to give this "parcel" to.

Infantile sexual theories

At the end of this clinical sequence, whose latent resources are fully illustrated by the associative contents, it certainly seemed that my decision not to interpret the dream about the business partner had allowed me to accompany Julien's attempt to approach the conflict aroused by his relationship with a castrating internal mother carrying inside her a dead object. It had of course not escaped me that this dream of seduction by the father was also the expression of his negative transference: was he not, after all, treating me openly as an "arse-licker"? I had nevertheless chosen not to refer the dream directly to his erotic homosexual transference, because at that juncture this would merely have reinforced his resistance to the conflict with the maternal imago.

The business-partner dream was one of the milestones that were to allow Julien in the ensuing sessions to address the conflict concerning a mother who aroused anxiety because she was castrated/castrating, filled with dead children—for him the equivalent of the father's faecalized penis (the "decapitated" head in the air raid). Already threatening by virtue of Julien's fantasy of castration and anal penetration, she became even more so in "climbing the ladder", thereby revealing her "bottom" to her son. This led him to discover what the "idealization" of the mother was protecting him from: she ceased to be a mother without instincts and became a woman who procreated, who took pleasure in procreating, a pleasure so intense that she "climbed all the way up the ladder"!

My question ("Did you not tell me in earlier sessions about something else as well . . .?") had had a binding effect, making for the emergence of a fantasy that structured (Viderman, 1970) an essential part of his relations with his internal parental objects, in that he had now become able to connect the weekend depression with the mention of the "dead children". This had also allowed the mother's traumatic, dead, and faecalized object to emerge, in the form of the decapitated head. This object was not that of Julien's ego, but had to do with his object's object. In that respect it was traumatic for him: the head represented an object which the mother, "having nothing to hold on to", had "seized hold of" with a view to handing it over to "someone" . . . This was probably because—at least, so I presume—she had experienced herself as "decapitated", hence castrated, at this traumatic moment.

Julien's representations had thus moved on from an instinctual "tidal-wave" mother, offering no protective shield against stimuli—a "rickety-hut" mother who created insecurity and offered no protection—to a traumatized/traumatizing mother, pregnant with a "decapitated head", the abortion of which constituted the active repetition of the trauma suffered. In the dream of the business partner, I became in the transference a condensation of his two parental imagos, a castrated father and a castrating mother, of whom the latter, having "lost her head", was pregnant with an object which for Julien represented the father's castrated and faecalized penis.

After recalling the scene of the air raid, the son, now the container for his mother's traumatic signifier, wished to hand this role over to me with respect to his internal mother, while at the same time seeking gradually to give up his reparative behaviour that would always prove ineffective unless he became an "arse-licker"—

which then confronted him with his own impotence and castration anxieties.

In these circumstances, the sole object of Julien's concern became the body. So it was that the anus came to represent a "castrated" neck—of the head (the "peculiar" sister, the hallucinating mother "climbing the ladder" and "losing" her head), of the baby (the abortion) and of the genital organs (the castration of the father, who had been "depressed" and had once had "suicidal ideas") all at the same time. As a result, the mother became castrated. It was then necessary for Julien to hand over the head of his internal mother to his analyst in order to restore the sequence of generations and an identity, a physical (bodily) reality. He handed himself over to someone who would allow him to resume possession of his body. If his mother was not a woman, because deprived of her head by castration (like an anus), then he himself could not be a boy who later would turn into a man. Seen in this light, the dream of the business partner had a reparative function at that particular point in time. Identified with his "castrated and headless" mother, he was asking me in the transference to "lick his anus". For him, the analyst became a twofold phallic object: first, a paternal object providing genital support and repairing the mother, and second, a representation of the little boy vainly attempting to "repair" his mother's castration with his tongue. His infantile sexual theory was thus revealed.

Psychic homosexuality and how it is "declined"

Thanks to some major texts by several French authors on this subject, I realized the fundamental significance in men of the structuring role of passive homosexuality as regards the relationship with the father, both in the construction of the psyche and in psychoanalytic treatment. In the latter situation, the degree of repression of the passive–feminine component bound up with psychic homosexuality in relation to a father figure is a vital reference point, which for some analysts can even be equated with an analytic "compass".

Unconscious psychic homosexuality, once a frequent stumbling block in psychoanalysis because it often caused patients to abandon their treatment, was a fundamental discovery that transformed the understanding of transference relationships and therapeutic technique. Latent homosexuality, expressed indirectly, used to give rise to a great deal of countertransference perplexity—not the least of which was Freud's experience as recorded in the famous note added in 1923 to the "Dora" analysis, quoted above. In the same year, Freud drew attention in *The Ego and the Id* to the structuring effects of the Oedipus complex on bisexuality (Freud, 1923b).

As Christian David has noted, the composite character of psychic bisexuality has to do

> not only with the complexity of its identifications but also with the bipolar components of its erotic and, more generally, affective fantasy structure, which is in turn under the influence of sexual reality and of all the aspects involved in the formation and functioning of the image of the body as a body possessing a specific sex and constituting the *locus* of instinctual sources. [David, 1975, p. 790]

Psychic homosexuality is thus an integral part of psychic bisexuality, whose own source lies both in conflictualized identifications and in early erotic and instinctual experiences, all these components being organizers of love-object choices. Psychic homosexuality can therefore be said to lie at the root or at the very heart of Oedipal structuring, its dynamics and its vicissitudes.

By concentrating on the structuring aspects of psychic homosexuality, I wish to emphasize a process the effects of which on the development of the transference can be observed. This process takes into account the history of the organization of the analysand's homosexual libidinal current. Psychic homosexuality is mostly implicit and unconscious. It is intimately bound up with both the organization and the whole problem complex of the feminine dimension and of masochism in the self, and consequently comes to reflect these.

1. The transference effects of psychic homosexuality are usually considered in two ways:
   (a) Defensive homosexuality due to regression—a retreat from the positive Oedipus complex and from the castration anxiety that heterosexuality entails. The result is a regressive identification with someone of the same sex; this identification

> is related to narcissistic libido cathecting an ideal object as a model. The dynamics are specifically anal, and the underlying fantasies involve both the wish to be and the fear of being penetrated. The main feature of the transference situation is homosexuality with the father. The erotic cathexis of the father, accompanied by passive submission, is of fundamental importance for establishing a therapeutic alliance in the analysis.
> (b) Primitive transference underlying homosexual-type defences. Traditionally, in the transference situation, cathexis of the erotic object and that of the ideal object are separate, although both remain under the primacy of phallic dynamics.

The ideal object constituting the model is a mythical character: the father of the primal horde, the father of one's personal prehistory (Freud, 1923b, p. 31). An image of the "primal mother" may be identified in the erotic object which, however, is *both* maternal *and* paternal, *having a specific sex* while at the same time being non-genitalized, the bearer of a universal sex known as the *phallus*. This sex is also an attribute of the phallic mother.

It is in this sense that these archaic regressive transferences are thought to relate to a primitive, phallic-narcissistic and omnipotent mother. For some authors, cathexis of the ideal object represented by the primal (phallic) father is possible only through the intermediary of a mother who carries inside her the phallic imago of the primal father. These authors therefore tend to see this kind of transference as *maternal* rather than as homosexual.

Other authors adopt a different approach and postulate the existence of a *primary homosexual instinct* (*primary homosexuality*), involving object-related libido. This primary homosexuality is said to determine the fate of homosexuality in psychic development. Primary homosexuality is a fantasy of identity which arises between the same-sex parent and the child, and organizes the transition from primary to secondary narcissism, a phase that lies between narcissistic cathexis of the self and cathexis of a non-self object. On emergence from primary identification it thus allows the self to acquire a specific-sex identity (Kestemberg, 1984), as well as permitting internalization of a primal scene fantasy, which thereupon furthers development of the self by integrating object-related auto-eroticism. Primary homosexuality, with its roots in the pre-Oedipal stage, thus stands in contrast to psychic bisexuality, which makes Oedipal development possible.

2. By invoking homosexual transference, we are at the same time defining the non-acceptance or non-integration of the feminine component and of the whole feminine dimension itself, in both men and women. The degree of repression of these feminine aspects is a very important parameter for the analysis and for prognosis, and can give a clue to the qualitative development of the psychoanalytic process.

Rejection of the feminine dimension ("repudiation of femininity", Freud, 1937c, p. 250) in both sexes may be the "bedrock" that stands in the way of analytic cure, the ultimate obstacle related to the need to repudiate the mother's feminine-ness, out of a fear that it might induce passivity in the self (Green, 1990).

Some authors consider that the organization and vicissitudes of the feminine dimension or of the feminine position in both boys and girls, in the context of the transformation of their bisexuality, take an anal–regressive course as a defence against integration of the *loci* of the feminine (vagina) and of the maternal (uterus) components (Bégoin-Guignard, 1984).

Non-integration of this dimension in both sexes gives rise to homosexual transferences in situations where we would normally not expect any—if we did not know from experience that regression in the psychoanalytic situation encourages regressive, pregenital and bi-valent transference. Because of castration anxiety, of the conflictuality associated with early maternal identifications, and of terrifying fantasies of being swallowed up which are organized around disavowal and splitting, these regressive types of transference are also fuelled by projections on to the analyst of condensed or combined pregenital images.

3. Finally, by invoking psychic homosexuality, we are also emphasizing the self's so-called "feminine" masochism. Its fantasy productions and economic fate, while common to both sexes, differ of course in their expression according to gender, i.e., the self's anatomical, identity-related, and identificatory sex. "Feminine" masochism, whose fantasy dynamics were

twice discussed by Freud (1919e, 1924c), enables the individual to regulate castration anxiety according to the paternal imago, anality, and phallic idealizations as the Oedipus complex is resolved.

In men, the active and central unconscious fantasy behind these dynamics is the incestuous link with the father, coupled with the need to repress the representation of the feminine position in relation to him that this implies. It is revealed in psychoanalytic treatment by the organization and development of the analysand's psychic homosexuality. Though the latter is an essential structuring position and has a fundamental organizing function, it is dependent on the unconscious fantasies that govern its creation. In Julien, for example, it was the weight and intensity of the representations connected with an *internal mother who was distressing and dangerous because she contained a dead, anal, and faecalized object, equivalent for him to female castration*, that led him to try to *interpose a paternal third entity* by means of his *homosexual erotic transference dream*. But he was then confronted with a *castrated father, an "arse-licker"*. It was my binding intervention—the question I asked not immediately but in the following session—that enabled him to hand over to me the traumatic maternal history and to de-condense representations of his mother. By way of a new paternal identification, he could *resume possession of his own body and identity by reintegrating the sequence of generations*. An infantile sexual theory focusing on his mother appeared as a backdrop to the dream. Had I been too quick in drawing attention to the homosexual element in the dream, I would have risked reinforcing the repression of his relationship and identifications both with an anally castrated father and with a traumatized, death-dealing mother.

That said, the essential question remains: is psychic homosexuality of the same nature, and does it perform the same function, in men and in women? After all, if the feminine dimension stems in both sexes from the original relationship with the mother, is the structuring homosexuality bound up with it organized around the same object in both boys and girls? Admittedly, men move on from their original relationship with the mother—one effect of this is to strengthen their feminine component—to secondary homosexuality with the Oedipal father. They then have to go through a psychic process (Bokanowski, 1993; Cournut-Janin & Cournut, 1993) leading up to the fantasy of the second phase of "A child is being beaten", the unconscious translation of which is: "My father loves me". It may be thought that in women there is no change of homosexual object as such, since girls are brought back to their maternal object each time. However, the primitive maternal object that includes the phallus does not offer girls the same kind of homosexual object relation as does the Oedipal maternal object. This situation is, furthermore, complicated by the organization of a homosexual phase more directly related to the father at the time of the phallic phase. For this reason, if we take the idea of psychic homosexuality in women to cover the same domain as its clinical and theoretical pattern in men, are we not coming close to a limiting concept—or at least the limits of the concept?

In adopting the concept of psychic homosexuality in both sexes, we should perhaps use the term in a plural form: not psychic homosexuality, but psychic homosexualities.

A mouse phobia

I shall now present an extract from the analysis of a female patient—I shall call her Jeanne—which, it seems to me, illustrates certain aspects of this proposition. As in the previous example, it hinges on a dream, the manifest content of which ran as follows: "She dreamt that she had babies, among which was a 'mouse baby'".

> Jeanne was a woman of twenty-five, an important feature of whose analysis was a trauma that had occurred during the Oedipal phase; this dream, which she reported when I returned after an absence, was the condensation of a whole sequence of her psychic history. Her father had had a very serious car accident, the sequellae of which were severe indeed. The prognosis made while he was in hospital was reserved in the extreme, and his condition had necessitated a long period in intensive care. Thereafter, and throughout Jeanne's childhood, the life of the family had been subjected to severe restrictions as a result of the father's state of health. On top of this, the mother had difficulty coping, and, often depressed, had made Jeanne feel that she could no longer be available for her. "Abandonment", "being let go of" and by extension "absence" were therefore the central themes around which Jeanne's analysis came to be organized.

So it was that, after a break due to one of my absences, Jeanne brought the dream in which *she had babies, among which was a "mouse baby"*. The signifier *mouse (souris* in French) aroused in her a whole series of representations, memories, and affects. Chief among these were the following:

1. The mice reminded her mainly—as in the dream—of *babies,* through the memory of a dissection in a school biology practical when she was a teenager. Her memories of this incident were extremely unpleasant because, when dissecting the uterus of a mouse preserved in formaldehyde, she had found it full of dead little mice ... She had then apparently fainted. Since this dissection, she had had a "phobia" of mice. This might also have to do with an unconscious fantasy of anal penetration and pregnancy. In a similar vein, the word *souris* (mouse) also reminded her of the "little mouse", i.e., losing her milk teeth[14] ("castration" and "void") and of reparation of the loss.

2. *Playing the little mouse* was one of her favourite fantasies. It was a listening fantasy that referred to the primal scene and to occasions in her childhood when she had shared the pleasure of listening to music with her father ... She had later satisfied her curiosity by playing this game, which had, however, one day taken a tragic turn, when she learned in this way of the death of her paternal grandmother and had heard her father cry for the first and only time in her life.

3. Again, the *souris* was associated with one of the most distressing memories of Jeanne's childhood. While her father was in the intensive care unit, she had gone to visit him with her mother. Her memory of this meeting was ghastly—traumatic in the true sense of the word. The sight of her father, lying motionless on a hospital bed, connected up to drips on all sides after a tracheotomy, unable to speak and barely conscious, had left her with a nightmarish memory, made all the more painful by the fact that, when the time came to leave her father, her mother had waved his paralysed hand as if to say "goodbye" to his daughter, at the same time saying "*Smile*[15] to Jeanne!" ...

In the session, I suggested to her that her mouse phobia could be interpreted as a possible displacement of a phobia of "babies" that had hitherto remained unconscious.

This reawakened Jeanne's memories of her younger sister, to whom she was very close. She remembered her mother's absence for the delivery and her return home, but had no memory of the baby or of how the new-born had been cared for.

In her associations, she then recalled the episode of the dissection: she had been twelve years old, anxiously awaiting her period. She had been worried about this event for at least a year and had constantly plied her mother with questions. Referring to her apprehensions, she then recalled having asked her mother to read with her the book her father had read to her when her sister was born, a book about the conception of children.

This could be understood as an unconscious homosexual wish, which, after repression, may have given rise to her phobic symptom.

The mother's body

At that point in the session, I said: "Could this have been a wish to have a child with your mother?"

This statement could be interpreted in two ways: (1) herself giving her mother a "baby" as her father had done, or (2) being made pregnant with a "baby" by her mother.

This shed light on a whole facet of her adolescent history: she remembered her first sexual experience, which had been homosexual, with a female cousin whom she had greatly idealized. This relationship had begun at the time of her parents' first long trip away after her father had partly recovered from his accident. Jeanne had experienced the absence of both of them as nothing less than an abandonment. The relationship with her cousin had continued for over a year; it had been followed by other liaisons of the same kind, which had come to an end more or less naturally when she had her first relationship with a boy. Analysis of these homosexual episodes revealed that, at the time of the physical and psychic changes of adolescence, Jeanne had been trying to achieve a better cathexis of her self-image and at the same time to rediscover her mother's body. This cathexis had been all the more necessary because her mother had been incapable of affective and sensual contact with her daughter, whereas Jeanne had told me how intensely she would have liked her mother to be the one who "revealed her femininity" to her.

To clarify this important movement, I shall summarize the situation briefly as follows:

1. The dream of the *mouse baby*, which reminded her of her phobia, came on my return from an absence.

2. The phobia had arisen during the dissection of the mouse pregnant with its dead babies; it had aroused in Jeanne the twofold wish to have a child by her mother and to kill the rival baby in the womb.
3. The onset of the phobia at the beginning of adolescence took her back to her homosexual fantasies and her primary relationship with her mother; these became even more meaningful with respect to the secondary homosexuality acted out during her adolescence.
4. That homosexuality had begun during her parents' first prolonged absence, which had revealed the partial failure of support from and internalization of her primary object relations.
5. This cast a singular light on Jeanne's purchase, some years earlier during our first long analytic separation for the summer holidays, of a sculpture representing the body of a woman, which she said she *liked to caress*. This was a continuation of the *erotic aspect of the primary relationship* with the maternal object, which I then represented in the transference and which she was afraid of losing because of my *absence*.

For Jeanne, having to forgo being the man capable of seducing her mother was, as in every girl, a necessary and structuring Oedipal development. In her case, however, this movement of identification with her father had been disrupted by the accident that had so disabled him. This had inflicted a terrible blow on her object both of Oedipal desire and of phallic identification, reinforcing her homosexual desire for the mother. This seems to be contained in the signifier *souris* (mouse/smile), which was a signifier with a number of different phallic valences. Symbolizing at one and the same time pregnancy (associated with a fantasy of anal penetration), reparation of loss (loss of a tooth) and the primal scene (playing the little mouse), with mourning for the father in the background (the father crying), it was primarily the rallying point for a traumatic fixation which included the absolute castration of the father: the ghastly memory of "*Souris* (smile) to Jeanne!"

The dream reflected the condensation of all these *souris* signifiers, transformed into a mouse-as-mammal-with-a-tail. This then enabled Jeanne, in her phallic identification with father, to penetrate into her mother's womb—but there she was liable to come across babies . . . dead little mice!

This dream, then, expressed the dramatic texture of the moment when Jeanne's psychic homosexuality became firmly established in the transference. Induced by my absence, the dream took her back to the primal scene between her parents, via their trip after the father's partial recovery from his road accident. In dreaming after my return that *she had babies, among which was a "mouse baby"*, she was identified with her mother in her wish to receive babies from the father. Also, however, through the *mouse baby*—the dead baby in the mother's womb—she was identified with the doubly castrated father: as an object of secondary identification (the disabled father unable to penetrate the mother) and, at the primary level, as a dead phallic object inside the mother's body (in accordance with the equation "penis = baby = faeces").

The partial failure of support from and internalization of her primary relationship with her mother, as revealed by the homosexual acting out in her adolescence, was transformed by the work of de-condensation and interpretation performed in connection with this dream.

The analysis of this clinical sequence, in which the various hues in the palette of her homosexuality found expression, illustrates how the concept of psychic homosexuality can throw light on the development of the transference–countertransference process.

A plurality of psychic homosexualities

Intimately bound up with the organization and development of psychic bisexuality in both sexes, and with the different strata that structure it, psychic homosexuality is a pattern which proves to be richly polysemous on both the conceptual and clinical levels. Since *The Ego and the Id* (Freud, 1923b), it has been regarded, in the dynamic movement of the Oedipus complex, as characteristic of identification with the same-sex parent's desired object.

In *boys*, where it is traditionally regarded as fundamental to the structuring role of passive homosexuality in the relationship with the father, psychic homosexuality is thus related to repression of the passive–feminine component.

In *girls*, in their relationship with the mother figure of the Oedipus complex, their psychic homosexual position represents the component of their masculine identification intended to seduce the mother. However, this accounts for only part of psychic homosexuality. It is an aspect of feminine-type homosexuality, in which the little girl wants to seduce her mother and receive a child from her. But there is also another constitutive factor of psychic homosexuality in girls, which belongs this time to the context of masculine-type homosexuality—that is to say, their secondary identification with the father and their wish to seduce him homosexually, after the fashion of the little boy who wishes to receive a big penis from father.

In boys, too, masculine and feminine aspects of homosexuality can likewise be distinguished. Their masculine-orientated homosexuality is underpinned by the wish to receive a big penis from the father (the little boy wants to seduce father and receive a big penis from him), while their feminine-orientated homosexuality, for its part, rests on the fantasy of receiving a child from him (after the fashion of the little girl who, like mother, wishes to receive a child from father).

The level of homosexual cathexes thus presents an asymmetry complementary to that which exists in homosexual cathexes of the Oedipus complex.

Again, the primary relationship with the mother is apparently a key factor in the organization of the feminine dimension, whose fate, as we know, is fundamentally different in boys and in girls. The origin of that component lies in the early relationships with the mother's body and mind; these relationships generate excitation yet at the same time represent a protective shield against over-stimulation. It is founded on the self's capacity for identification with the mother's feminine side. What I have defined as feminine-type homosexuality in the context of psychic homosexuality may, therefore, in the secondary version of the negative form of the Oedipus complex, be its expression.

In conclusion, I suggest that psychic homosexuality should be spoken of not in the singular but in the plural.

With regard to the clinical aspects of this plural psychic homosexuality, its investigation in two patients (one male, the other female) led me to rethink certain technical parameters relevant to the form, content and timing of interpretations. In the case of the male patient, I felt it better to postpone interpreting a manifest aspect of his homosexual dream, and this allowed the underlying triangulation and associated primal fantasies to appear in the dynamics of the treatment. With the female patient, an interpretation that put into words the implicit homosexual texture of her dream was the factor that reopened the way to a possible triangular conflictualization. When interpreting psychic homosexuality, it is necessary to bear in mind all its component parameters. Failing this, the analyst may well lock himself into a defensive countertransference movement that could then cause him to ignore any interpretative reference to primal fantasies, to avoid the physical and psychic dimension of the primary relationship, and to short-circuit triangulation, the difference between generations and the twofold valence—both relational and identificatory—of the relationship with the object.

III Working on bisexuality in analysis: the feminine dimension in men

> The more the work of the past year recedes into perspective, the better pleased I am with it. Now for bisexuality! I am sure you are right about it. And I am accustoming myself to the idea of regarding every sexual act as a process in which four persons are involved. We shall have a lot to discuss about that. [Letter 113, dated 1 August 1899, from Freud to Fliess]

The final chapter of "Analysis terminable and interminable" (Freud 1937c)—a paper which, as I have already said, can be regarded as Freud's last will and testament with respect to the practice of psychoanalysis—raises the question of obstacles lying in the path of the psychoanalytic process, together with that of the therapeutic effectiveness of psychoanalysis. Freud discusses the difficulties the analyst encounters in the course of an analysis, in particular such factors of resistance as (in female patients) the "envy for the penis" and (in men) the "struggle against (their) passive or feminine attitude" (*ibid.*, p. 250). Raising the question of the capacity for and degree of psychic internalization of femininity and of the feminine position *in both sexes*, Freud writes:

> At no other point in one's analytic work does one suffer more from an oppressive feeling that all one's repeated efforts have been in

> vain, and from a suspicion that one has been "preaching to the winds", than when one is trying to persuade a woman to abandon her wish for a penis on the ground of its being unrealizable or when one is seeking to convince a man that a passive attitude to men does not always signify castration and that it is indispensable in many relationships in life. [*ibid.*, p. 252]

Thus, for Freud, the evolution of the organization of psychic bisexuality and its management during the psychoanalytic process is one of the keys to the outcome of analysis. Consequently, the "bedrock" constituted by the "repudiation of femininity"—or even its "disavowal"—is one of the major issues at stake in any analytic treatment:

> It would be hard to say whether and when we have succeeded in mastering this factor in an analytic treatment. We can only console ourselves with the certainty that we have given the person analysed every possible encouragement to re-examine and alter his attitude to it. [*ibid.*, pp. 252–253]

Psychoanalytic treatment and psychic bisexuality

It is customary to define the analytic space as a specific *locus* that allows the analysand's transference neurosis—or transference psycho-neurosis—to develop and be analysed by the psychoanalyst.

The analytic space is therefore a *locus* in which the dynamics of the process are based on a convergence between two mental spaces: that of the patient, whose *transference* traditionally develops and organizes a neurosis called transference neurosis (or psycho-neurosis), and that of the analyst with his or her *countertransference*, i.e., resistance to the patient's transference.

Though the affects generated in the transference neurosis and in the analyst's countertransference differ as to their dynamics and expressive quality, both contribute to the structuring of the analytic space.

In the wider sense of the term, the countertransference is traditionally defined as the affects experienced by the analyst in working with the patient and with the latter's transference. The countertransference is a mechanism inherent to the analytic situation and represents one of the most important instruments for the psychoanalyst's thinking and interpretative work. Whether the countertransference is the expression of the analyst's instinctual experience as regards the patient's transference or that of the analyst's general endeavours to work on the material, it is a component of the psychoanalytic process *per se*, given the identificatory and counter-identificatory implications involved.

More specifically, the analysis of the patient's resistances—related to transference reactions that are all the more intense and evocative because of their repetitive aspect in the patent's history—and the analysis of the defensive manoeuvres prompted by the transference neurosis are both, for the analyst, constantly present in the work of every analysis. In other words, the effects of the patient's resistance *in addition to* that of the analyst (*counter-resistance*), each related to its respective affects, give impetus to the psychoanalytic process.

The nuclear complex of the neuroses—the *Oedipus complex*—is the crucial structuring element of the psyche, the guiding principle, the backbone and the driving force behind every psychoanalytic treatment. It organizes the psychic conflictuality linked, in each of us, to our instinctual dynamics, desires, and identifications. It is the source of energy that fuels the process of individuation, and it lies at the heart of the symbolic organization of the castration complex that expresses the twofold conflictuality regarding the difference between the sexes and that between generations. As an expression of how desires and anxieties circulate, located and enmeshed at various levels of the mind, it covers the whole range of identificatory positions related to working through psychic bisexuality.

The Oedipus complex is always twofold in nature—positive and negative forms—and leads to a double identification, masculine *and* feminine. These two types of identification, governed by the castration complex, do not have the same force—since one dominates and more or less masks the other, they are simultaneously complementary and contradictory. On this point, in *The Ego and the Id*, Freud wrote:

> It would appear, therefore, that in both sexes the relative strength of the masculine and feminine sexual dispositions is what determines whether the outcome of the Oedipus situation shall be an

> identification with the father or with the mother. This is one of the ways in which bisexuality takes a hand in the subsequent vicissitudes of the Oedipus complex. The other way is even more important. [. . .] Closer study usually discloses the more complete Oedipus complex, which is twofold, positive and negative, and is due to the bisexuality originally present in children: that is to say, a boy has not merely an ambivalent attitude towards his father and an affectionate object-choice towards his mother, but at the same time he also behaves like a girl and displays an affectionate feminine attitude to his father and a corresponding jealousy and hostility towards his mother. [Freud, 1923b, p. 33]

The Oedipus complex crops up all through life in different modes of psycho-sexual functioning and, in psychoanalytic treatment, is always being called into question and worked over again and again. Given the patient's early internal and external object-related identifications and the identificatory conflicts linked to the evolution of the Oedipal situation, with its twofold (positive and negative) valence, the transference therefore embodies a double psychic and sexual polarity that develops in the course of the psychoanalytic process.

It is therefore quite clear that the Oedipus complex is crucial to the work done on bisexuality in the analysis for both protagonists in the psychoanalytic situation, patient and analyst.

Though the countertransference, of course, is not simply a reduplication that seeks to "counter" the transference, psychoanalysis does all the same put to the test the analyst's own identifications and psychic bisexuality. In any given session, the latter is constantly placed in jeopardy, at the level of deeply-unconscious identifications, by the interplay of a twofold (topographical and formal) regressive movement, as well as by the arousal of the fantasy activity at the heart of the analyst's "infantile" dimension involving organizing and working through his or her infantile sexual theories. This implies that the part played by infantile sexual theories in establishing intrapsychic representations of sexuality—and, more precisely, of bisexuality—is a dominant one.

If the analyst enjoys a certain degree of freedom with respect to his or her pre-conscious fantasy life, woven on the loom of infantile theories of sexuality, it becomes possible to use these in a positive manner with some degree of internal freedom. This enables the analyst to identify with other people and their specific differences—in particular with someone of the opposite sex or someone who has a significantly different psycho-sexual make-up. For this to occur, the analyst must have integrated bisexuality sufficiently well and be able to cope "fully" with how it functions.

Some degree of stability is therefore necessary to keep abreast of the various analytic features the patient attributes to the analyst in the transference. To some extent, the analyst's instrument is his or her own self, i.e., the instinctual forces that are unconsciously at work in the countertransference dynamics and have to be "dealt with" as the analyst's attention remains focused on the patient. This raises the issue of the fate of the primal fantasies from which these forces are derived, and the fate of the accompanying infantile sexual theories that represent them.

From time to time the analyst comes up against an internal impossibility to come fully to terms with his or her own bisexuality. When this occurs, the resulting blind spot in the countertransference relationship may deflect and modify the psychoanalytic process—or perhaps even bring it to a halt.

Freud gave a famous example of this in the note he added in 1923 to the "Dora" analysis: "Before I had learnt the importance of the homosexual current of feeling in psychoneurotics, I was often brought to a standstill in the treatment of my cases or found myself in complete perplexity" (Freud, 1905e, n. 120). Freud admitted that the interruption of certain analyses was essentially due to the fact that, at the time, he was not able to bear being the object—or the eventual aim—of a feminine homosexual transference, and even less the idea of being the "source" of such a transference (Neyraut, 1974). It was only several years later that Freud acknowledged that Dora's analysis ended the way it did because at that time he was himself unable to interpret her homosexual transference. We now know that he would have been able to make such an interpretation only on condition that he could at that point see himself in the guise of a feminine (homosexual) object—in other words, had he been able, in his countertransference, to identify with a woman.

Consequently, as Christian David has pointed out (David, 1992), psychic bisexuality lies at the very heart of the analyst's work—the crux of the work *of* the countertransference as well as that *on* the countertransference. This, as de Urtubey (1994) suggests, is the distinctive feature of psychoanalysis in the true sense of the word.

Working on bisexuality

Psychoanalysts do not deal with sexuality as such, but with the complex forms that its representations adopt in their polysemous diversity.

With regard to these representations in psychoanalysis, sexual identity and gender identity, male and female, have their roots in the schemata and bodily experiences that are reflected in an individual's genetic sex and anatomical sex.

If psychic bisexuality, as an echo of the self's multiple identifications, corresponds to his or her anatomical and physiological characteristics, the incestuous fantasy dynamics that govern psychic bisexuality do none the less give it a particular flavour.

These unconscious fantasy dynamics need not correspond entirely to the self's sexual reality; they depend to some extent on certain features that constitute the psychic structure of the self, including the highly important factor of identification with the opposite sex.

Given the history of an individual's unconscious identifications with his or her objects, everything that derives from the instinctual drives must be more or less related to psychic bisexuality. Analysis enables certain former identificatory tendencies to come to the fore, develop and be re-sexualized thanks to their being "re-bisexualized" (David, 1992) in the transference relationship underpinned by imaginary relationships with past objects.

The effects such identifications have on the analysand's narcissism and object-related valences will be very different, depending on whether they involve same-sex or opposite-sex objects. As a result, the psychoanalytic situation is a test of specific psychosexual identity, while at the same time stimulating psychic bisexuality. This twofold impact requires some work to be done on the economics of the instinctual drives: regression of psychosexual uncertainty, identity re-structuring, and a greater degree of flexibility as to primary and secondary identificatory cathexes and counter-cathexes. Due to the regressive modalities inherent to psychoanalysis (formal, topographical, and temporal), the treatment may turn out to be "de-constructing"; the resistances that are difficult to overcome do not always lead to the perspective of a genuinely new integration of psychosexual dynamics.

Pregenital bisexuality

As we know, in the primary relationship with the mother, there is a close correspondence between the emergence of desire, the genesis and development of fantasy, the construction of internal objects and the organization of identifications that, stage by stage, come to constitute the elements of psychic bisexuality. Hence, bisexuality is an indicator of the internalization of the active–passive polarity, of the gradual introjection of sexual polarity and of the unconscious process of bisexualization that, since identifications and their vicissitudes go hand in hand, is operating somewhere in the background.

The nature, importance, and quality of the links between the individual and his or her primary objects will make for more or less flexibility in the capacity to play with—and therefore take pleasure in—the identificatory potentiality of bisexuality.

In their genital expression, psychic processes naturally make use of the resources of bisexuality, both defensively and for purposes of satisfaction. These two alternating movements will support each other all the more easily if the individual's bisexuality is able to dialogue in some degree of harmony with the different agencies that govern how it functions. Also, bisexuality will be all the more "internalized" if it manages to integrate into its own functioning the pregenital components of sexuality.

This, however, is not always the case. Pregenital forms of bisexuality sometimes over-develop because they have become caught up in a conflict relationship with the primary objects. This does not make for a harmonious internalization of bisexuality, nor for the flexibility that the genitalized expression of identificatory interplay requires.

When pregenital forms of bisexuality emerge in session material, they are usually quite difficult to identify. Given the fact that they are caught up in narcissistic conflicts indicative both of hatred for and stubborn attachment to the object, they are expressed mainly in terms of a certain imprecision of ego-boundaries. Related to anxiety over emptiness and nothingness—sometimes transformed into catastrophic anxiety—they generate confusion both in the relationship between inside and outside, and as between the erotogenic zones. At times like these, the patient's communications are expressed in a "non-sexual" way that puts the sense of identity under tremendous threat. This confusion masks infantile sexuality and makes it difficult to identify the problem complex involving desire, so that the analyst's countertransference is subjected to considerable pressure.

Several parameters thus come into play in the organization of the analyst's way of understanding psychic bisexuality in the patient. Masculine and feminine dimensions of infantile sexuality (as well as of adult sexuality) give rise to a whole range of expressions—pregenital and genital, homosexual and heterosexual, paternal, maternal, and infantile—within the transference relationship.

Let us take as an example the case of a male psychoanalyst with a male patient. At the most manifest level, the psychoanalyst, a man (father, brother, son), will have to listen to the masculine (father, brother, son) traits of another man. He will also be confronted, as a man, with the feminine (mother, sister, daughter) aspects of this other man.

At a more latent level, he will be attentive to his patent's masculine tendencies directed towards the analyst as a feminine transference object; this, from the countertransference point of view, leads the analyst to function in terms of his own feminine identifications.

His troubles are not yet over, however, because—*last, not least*—he will be confronted in the transference with a situation in which he, as a woman, will be in touch with the feminine tendencies of his male patient.

It is obvious, then, that the identificatory positions as regards both protagonists in the analysis have fundamentally to do with the problem of the feminine dimension in men.

I shall try now to illustrate these hypotheses by means of a few extracts taken from the analysis of a male patient with a male psychoanalyst. The sessions demonstrate the reciprocal involvement of each participant's unconscious feminine positions, show how these are mobilized and indicate how, after interpretation, they develop in such a way as to enable the patient to become aware of an unconscious fantasy on which was based one aspect of his infantile sexual theories.

The unthinkable prospect of a feminine desire in men

As I mentioned in the previous section, Julien undertook analysis in order to clarify the reasons behind his feelings of widespread dissatisfaction in his relationships both with his immediate circle and with his own self. The central theme of his analysis was the discovery of a relatively severe latent depression that appeared to have begun in early childhood.

Before coming to analysis, he had never show any signs of depression. In other words, he did not consult me for symptoms that might have required a course of treatment specifically aimed at depression—it was the analysis itself that uncovered his infantile depression. The extracts I present here are taken from sessions during a single week of the analysis.

> In the first session of that week, Julien told me of a conversation he had overheard the previous day, in which the incredible "power" of "non-orthodox" analysts practising "short" and "variable-length" sessions was being denounced. Julien, however, had thought of the "incredible power that patients have over their orthodox analysts", given that during a single fixed-length session—which lasts for quite some time—they could think and talk of "everything", whatever their analyst's "state of mind" and "internal availability".
>
> With respect to how the transference was developing, I felt that in bringing up these issues Julien was referring explicitly to the analyst's capacity to take in his patient's projections—in other words, to the *feminine and receptive qualities of the analyst's bisexuality*.
>
> I commented on the parallel between the "power" he feared yet desired to wield over me and what had previously been worked on in the analysis concerning his fantasy of dominating a mixed-race woman friend of his, whose skin colour attracted him sexually. The basis for his arousal was his anal–sadistic fantasies of possessiveness, principally related to having "power over other people" that went almost as far as "enslaving" them. Julien and I knew that the essential function of these fantasies was to protect him not only from his tender feelings towards this woman friend but also from those which he feared she might have for him.
>
> "I hadn't thought of the parallel between my friend and you," he replied—adding, all the same, that he sometimes arranged to meet her either shortly before or shortly after his sessions with me.

He associated to the fact that the previous day he had found himself thinking of me in the context of the discussion about psychoanalysts. He was struck by that fact, because until then he had never consciously thought about me, nor about the analysis, between sessions. I then reminded him of a childhood memory he had often brought up during his sessions: whenever, as a schoolboy, he made objects (ashtrays, decorated plates, alabaster figurines, etc.) or drawings, he would destroy them—and thereby get rid of them—on his way home. I commented that "he seemed to be treating me and his sessions in the same way as he used to treat the objects and drawings he made in school". After this comment, Julien remained silent for several minutes.

He broke the silence to say, just before the end of the session, that he felt "blocked" by something he couldn't bring himself to tell me.

Though I could not make any precise guess as to what this was, Julien's silence and his feeling of being "blocked" seemed to me at that point to have something to do with the various parallels we had drawn in the session, in so far as they had reawakened certain conflicts related to unconscious aspects of his homosexual transference.

The following day, Julien tackled what he had said he could not bring himself to tell me in the previous session.

He had gone to see his woman friend, the mixed-race lady, the week before, and had had sex with her. Thereafter, he had realized that his condom had burst; his first thought was of the risk of contamination by the AIDS virus. His partner, who did not seem particularly worried, had tried to reassure him—but, ever since that moment, it had preyed on his mind.

I pointed out that his "blocking" had occurred the previous day, after I had drawn a parallel between how he treated me in his thoughts and the way he used to destroy objects he had made in school. I added, "It's as though, in making this parallel, I had forced you to face up to my presence inside you, something that would appear to prey on your mind."

That comment enabled us to understand that he would try to contact his woman friend whenever he felt *depressed* in the hours immediately before or after his sessions.

"As though to get rid of me and the depressive feelings that the sessions reawaken?" I asked.

Julien agreed, and went on to talk at some length about the sadness that used to overwhelm him as a child or adolescent whenever his father gave him the impression that he (his father) was not particularly receptive to or available for him.

Though Julien and I had already discussed and tried to work through the theme of destruction/evacuation of his objects from an anal point of view (holding in/disposing of), it seemed to me that, thanks to the various parallels I had suggested in the previous session, the theme we had discussed and analysed over and over again was now in fact taking on a different slant in the transference, namely the following two aspects:

- first, his fear that deep inside himself he might suddenly feel both the wish to have tender feelings towards me and the wish that I might prove more receptive and available than his father had been in the past;
- and, above all, his refusal to put himself in a feminine position with respect to me that might lead him to desire and to fear being "impregnated" by my interpretations.

In the third session of the week, Julien said he would have liked to continue with what we had been discussing previously, but in the interval something had happened that had "staggered" him.

The day before, one of his male friends had spoken very openly to him about an extra-marital relationship that the friend's mother had kept up for some time because it had meant a great deal to her. Julien was "flabbergasted" by the apparently natural manner in which his friend had talked of his mother's sentimental and sexual life.

I said: "In other words, that a mother can have feelings for a man and be sexually active?"

Julien avoided all association to his own mother; instead, he spoke about "Lucy", the Australopithecus female discovered in Tanzania: "The original mother, the African female with a capital 'A', the mother of all mankind," he said. The 'African female' led him to associate to his mixed-race woman friend and to the fear of Aids that had haunted him since the episode of the burst condom.

I made a comment in relation to his earlier association: "The fear of being contaminated by the AIDS virus ('flabbergasted'[16]) or that of having impregnated the woman he associated with the 'original mother'?"

Julien replied that there was something else he had not yet mentioned. After the condom incident, his woman friend had said to him by way of a joke: "I hope you haven't given me twins". Deep down, he had been delighted by that remark. Why twins? Julien did not know, but the idea pleased him.

I said: "Perhaps the fact that in making twins you would feel twice as powerful?", then added: "Twice as powerful as your father?"

Julien's thoughts turned back to Lucy and to the idea that she seemed to be the "origin" of all mankind.

What he said about this idea gave me the impression that he was getting rid of everything that had to do with the instinctual aspect of impregnation and procreation—in other words, the fact that this situation implies a woman desiring a male partner.

With reference to the material in the two earlier sessions—the "incredible power patients have over orthodox analysts" and the danger represented by the desire *of* and *for* the "original mother" (Lucy the African, his mixed-race friend, me in the transference)—it seemed that Julien was getting rid both of his feminine wish to be impregnated by me and of his fear of my feminine wish to be impregnated by him.

By associating AIDS with the fear of being in a feminine position in which he could be sexually aroused and impregnated by me, Julien was expressing his fear of homosexuality—hence his resistance with respect to introjection and the need he had felt as a child to destroy the objects he created.

At the same time, this fantasy offered him some protection against his wish to exercise "incredible power" over me: his imagined possessiveness (Denis, 1997) explains both his unconscious fantasy of wanting to impregnate me twice as powerfully as his father (twins) as well as the castration anxiety connected with this fantasy.

This highlights Julien's difficulties as regards pregenital bisexuality; they prevented his "playing" with his structuring psychic homosexuality (see the previous section). He was therefore afraid to identify with a desiring and impregnable mother *and* had to avoid the idea that I might, in his eyes, represent such a desiring and impregnable mother.

Thus, the more he refused or resisted the feeling of being impregnated in a feminine position by my transference interpretations and comments, the stronger was the pressure for a return of the repressed under the guise of a wish for/fear of his "unthinkable" masculine power to impregnate me.

I proposed an interpretation along these lines; Julien thereupon fell silent for several minutes.

When he came out of his silence, he said he had been thinking that he did indeed feel a need to destroy my comments and interpretations. I pointed out that he said this after the long comment I had made . . . as though, perhaps, he was trying to destroy me.

Julien laughed. The session ended at that point.

In his final session of the week, Julien reported a dream in which *he was sticking together two pieces of a broken plate*. He associated to the fact that, the previous evening, he had watched a television programme about the reunification of East and West Germany after the Berlin Wall was demolished. Then he associated to his parents who had separated and whom he was unable to bring together again in his life.

The transference dynamics worked through during the week thus reached the point where Julien seemed able to tolerate the pain involved in "reuniting" in his mind his internal parents, his paternal and maternal, masculine and feminine identifications.

My psychoanalytic work of interpretation, derived from acceptance and working through of my own feminine position seemed to have helped Julien to diminish the splitting he had set up with respect to his bisexuality and to stop taking refuge exclusively in the search for a *neuter gender* (Green, 1973).

The feminine dimension in men

As Christian David puts it, the composite character of psychic bisexuality

> reflects not only the complexity of the identifications involved, but also the bipolar components of the erotic—and indeed emotional—fantasy world that is itself influenced by sexual reality and by all the other elements that participate in the formation and functioning of the image of the body as possessing a specific sex, *locus* and source of the instinctual drives. [David, 1975]

The fact of being a girl implies that one's bodily and mental experiences will differ from those of a boy throughout life (the opposite is of course equally true). Though experience and fantasy cannot be subsumed one within the other, it remains true none the less that experience is what gives psychic reality its feeling of being actually lived through. In other words, the difference between the sexes related to anatomical sex, to bodily experience and to mental activity (fantasy integration) becomes greater as the Oedipal situation unfolds.

In children, the structuring of bisexuality is related to that of each of the parents. As Green (1975) has pointed out: "It is not the other person's sex that is represented in bisexuality, but the idea that one builds up of the other's sex from the point of view of one's own sex and from what one's own sex reads in the way the other sex looks upon it".

It follows logically that the masculine dimension in women is not of the same nature as that in men, just as the feminine dimension in men is not the same as that in women (Cournut-Janin & Cournut, 1993). However, as I mentioned at the outset, what is common to both sexes is their *rejection of the feminine dimension*—though the consequences are different for each sex, since this refusal affects women in the sex they have and men in the sex they do not have.

Given this refusal, it is all the more difficult to understand and define the concept of the feminine dimension in men since the specifically feminine component involved in integrating something into the mind is usually recognized only when it fails to work—or when its effects can be identified in successful cases of sublimation. As we saw with Julien, it is mainly the inadequacies or contradictions in the harmonious internalization of bisexuality that enable us very gradually to address in men certain failures in their attempt to integrate the feminine dimension.

As is well known, the fate of this dimension in men is fundamentally different from that in women. In the Oedipal situation, the boy recovers an object of the same sex as his primary object, whereas the girl, who has to change her object, must give up her original cathexis in order to turn towards—then take refuge in—a relationship with the father. Nevertheless, her future identity and destiny as a woman is built around her introjective identification with the mother's feminine dimension, a prelude to her subsequent identification with the mother's genital femininity.

But what about boys? What vicissitudes influence *their* feminine component once they reach the point of disengagement from their primary identification with the mother's feminine dimension? What happens to this femininity to make it so much of a problem?

One of the main difficulties in trying to outline the modalities that structure the feminine dimension and its vicissitudes in men seems basically to have to do with the fact that, in men, the feminine dimension is subjected to a double imprint, a double destiny and a double logic (Bokanowski, 1993).

A rough outline of this change would run as follows:[17]

- the primary object encourages both boys and girls to move in the direction of a primary identification with the maternal feminine dimension; the boy, in constant contact with his mother, introjects her primary maternal and feminine components and identifies with them (Bégoin-Guignard, 1988). In this first stage, mother and son "nourish" each other—the mother feeds on her son's libido that establishes her as a mother, the son on the introjective components of his mother's maternal and feminine libido;
- in this first stage, the boy identifies with his mother, who acknowledges him as a human being with a specific sex and sees him as a boy. Given that this relationship is between two people who are different-and-not-similar, it is easy to imagine the complex nature of the boy's primary identification with the maternal feminine dimension;
- this stage is also the time when the child establishes a psychic matrix and develops auto-eroticism through interactions related to primary homosexuality (Kestemberg, 1984);
- the next stage is that of the loss of the primary object, equivalent to what Green calls "cutting the psychic umbilical cord"; this is when mourning for the primary object takes place, with the arrival of the depressive position;
- this in turn generates awareness of the father as the object's Other. For the child, this implies the advent of the father in the early Oedipal situation—the father as manifested through the (female) lover's censorship (Braunschweig & Fain, 1975), present in the mother's Oedipal thinking. The father is thus established in the *third position* (Britton, 1989, 2004, p. 48), thus both separating and remaining present as a potential love object;

- henceforth, the pre-Oedipal identification with the father becomes organized, thereby enabling the boy to de-indentify with imagos of the phallic mother, to identify with the genital masculinity of the father and hence to consolidate his own masculine dimension. The feminine component is no longer governed simply by identification with the maternal feminine dimension—it is structured with respect to the father and directly aimed at him;
- the son's feminine and tender impulses which until that point were mainly directed towards the mother's tenderness, are henceforth aimed at the father's tenderness. The road is therefore open for establishing the beginnings of secondary homosexuality that both organizes the Oedipal situation and—because of the Oedipal effects of the castration complex—is a consequence of it.

I would therefore suggest that, just as girls change their object in going from mother to father then take refuge in the Oedipus complex, the feminine dimension in boys also changes its object in going from mother to father.

Two possible outcomes for the feminine dimension in men: psychic homosexuality and masochism

The question that now falls to be answered is the following: when we speak of the feminine dimension in men, what exactly do we mean by that term? The primary feminine component related to primary identification with the maternal feminine dimension—which, according to some, is the only true one—or, perhaps, as Winnicott maintained, part of an element he called "pure female" (Winnicott, 1966[1989, p. 173]) that is found in both sexes as a result of primary "non-instinctual" identification with the breast (Winnicott, 1971)? Or again, the feminine dimension involved in the negative or inverted mode of the Oedipus complex, related to the position in the boy's mind with respect to the father, specifically in terms of the ongoing processes of the castration complex—which, as a result, uses passivity to push to the forefront a defensive type of femininity?

These questions are not unrelated, for primitive—and, even more, pregenital—phenomena connect them together, and this fact too generates a certain number of consequences.

Bisexuality, psychic homosexuality and the transference

Traditionally, the tendency is to consider the feminine dimension in men only in terms of the modalities specific to the negative (inverted) form of the Oedipus complex (through the defensive passive position adopted with respect to the father) that "declines" as the Oedipus complex itself "declines" or "dissolves" following three syntagms (I shall put them in the simplest possible way):

- The structuring inverted form of the Oedipus complex. This was the one Freud described in the analysis of Little Hans and, to some extent, in that of the Rat-man;
- The regressive inverted Oedipus complex. This occurs when the pregenital forms of bisexuality are foremost. Freud encountered this type of Oedipal situation in his analysis of the Wolf-Man;
- The situation described by Freud in *Leonardo da Vinci and a Memory of his Childhood* (1910c). This refers to the problem of narcissistic identification with a phallic mother together with the (apparent) exclusion of the father from the mental sphere. A completely different syntagma, the homothetic inverse of the latter, relates to the struggle against a phallic-narcissistic maternal imago that is intrusive and destructuring; this situation can lead to the delusional trans-sexual and transforming position described by Freud in his discussion of the case of Senatspräsident Schreber (1911c).

In their mental development, all men go through these three stages at one point or another, though only one "fundamental" erotogenic zone acts as a pivot for arousal and representation: the anal and rectal zone (which, in boys, is not "leased out to the vagina" (Freud, 1917c, p. 133) but to the father's penis).

This is where we rejoin the impact of primitive (and particularly pregenital) phenomena—at the junction between anal and anality, the hub where all the difficult negotiations take place between such pairings as activity/passivity, container/contained, control/letting go, etc. These negotiations foreshadow and organize the essential feature for men, that of the *pars pro toto*.

This description covers both forms of masculine homosexuality mentioned in the previous chapter, those that further our understanding of the transference effects of psychic homosexuality via bisexuality: defensive homosexuality through regression as regards the positive form of the Oedipus complex, and the primitive transference that underlies homosexual-type defences.

Also, as we have seen, for some authors the rejection of the feminine dimension represents the ultimate barrier involved in the need to repudiate the mother's feminine component in case it drives the self in the direction of passivity (Green, 1990). For others, the organization and vicissitudes of the feminine dimension or position in boys, as regards dealing with bisexuality, follow the anal-regressive path as a defence against integrating specifically feminine (vagina) and maternal (uterus) *loci* (Bégoin-Guignard, 1988).

It would therefore seem to be the case that non-acceptation and non-integration of the feminine component and dimension generate a homosexual transference in the most unexpected of situations—even though we know that the regression produced because of the psychoanalytic situation generates regressive, pregenital and bivalent kinds of transference. However, the extent to which the feminine component and dimension are repressed is an important indicator of the psychoanalytic process as it develops in the analysis and of the likely prognosis for the patient.

So-called "feminine" masochism in men

Apart from psychic homosexuality (and its defensive variations related to how bisexuality is handled), the other possible outcome of the feminine question in men goes under the name of "feminine" masochism. Though its fantasy products and economic fate are common to both sexes, the way these are expressed depends, of course, on the sex of the individual concerned—anatomical, identity-related, and identificatory.

The fantasy dynamics of "feminine" masochism were highlighted on two occasions by Freud (1919e, 1924c), who showed how it enabled the individual to adapt castration anxiety to the paternal imago, anality and phallic idealization as the Oedipus complex diminished in intensity. In men, the incestuous link with the father and the need to repress representations of the feminine position with respect to the father constitute the principal unconscious fantasy in operation.

It is true that the basic feminine-masochistic fantasy in "A child is being beaten" (in the second phase: "My father is beating me, my father loves me") sheds considerable light on the child's position with respect to paternal *violence*, which is simultaneously dreaded, admired and envied (Green, 1986a). It is because the child longs for this kind of violence that he tries to take it over for himself in a regressive way. The "characteristically female situation", with its reference to "being castrated, or copulated with, or giving birth to a baby" (Freud, 1924c, p. 162), thus opens on to a fantasy of appropriation by introjecting the "non-castratable" and omnipotent paternal penis.

It is none the less possible to see in the fantasy of a child being beaten a metamorphosis that gives shape to a primal fantasy of seduction of a child by an adult (including the mother). The child has the experience of being the mother's sexual object and participates fully—though passively—in her pleasure, feeling him- or herself to be the mother's privileged pleasure-giving instrument; recourse to this fantasy is a way for the mind actively to control and "bind" its excitation so as to disengage from the depths of "primary seduction" and the endemic passivity—source of terror—it entails. The fantasy of a child being beaten is not only an attempt to re-establish unity with the mother but also a way of protecting the child from fantasies of being fused, engulfed, swallowed up and annihilated by the mother's presence—since the father beating the child comes between them in his role as third-party. Nevertheless, faced with the threat to his penis—in other words, to his narcissism—implied in the boy's passive–erotic relationship with the father, the fantasy "my father is beating me" (in other words, "my father loves me") changes into "my mother is the one who is beating me" (the third stage in the fantasy of "A child is being beaten").

For boys, then, a feminine dimension is opened up by the mother through primary feminine and maternal identification; however, as we have seen, it brings in its wake terrifying fantasies involving fusion, being made passive and being swallowed up . . .

The "beaten child" fantasy offers boys a more tolerable internalization of the "feminine component" that is part of the primary relationship with the mother, since it also allows for several kinds of declension:

- on the one hand, as we have just seen, behind the latent meaning of the fantasy "my father is beating me", under cover of being beaten by the father, the point is clearly to regain unity with the mother;
- on the other hand, through anal introjection of the father's penis—under cover of the "characteristically female situation" ("being castrated, or copulated with, or giving birth to a baby" (Freud, 1924c, p. 162))—the fantasy enables a much more direct Oedipal access to the mother.[18]

Hence, as a backdrop to the simultaneously instinctual and defensive interaction that activates the central fantasy "my father is beating me", the same kind of object change as that described above concerning the feminine dimension in men again appears here.

The feminine dimension as a focal point of analysis

Since this component is in its own right a part of psychic bisexuality and structures this crucial dimension governing the whole psycho-sexual and libidinal development in human beings, it is indeed at the very heart of the psychoanalytic process.

Whatever the psychic modalities (borrowed psychic clothing) adopted by resistance to this feminine component in the psychoanalytic relationship (psychic homosexuality, masochism, etc. . . .), it would seem that the source, in men, of their rejection or even "disavowal" of the feminine dimension lies, firstly, in the need to repudiate this aspect in the mother (because of the fear that it will result in complete passivity of the self) and, secondly, in the defence against internalizing the *loci* specific to the feminine (vagina) and maternal (uterus) spheres.

If the analyst listening to his or her patient does not focus sufficiently on the transference modalities associated with the patient's bisexuality (and on the countertransference modalities associated with the analyst's own bisexuality) as well as on the sexual theories that underpin them, the analysis may well founder on the "bedrock" represented by "repudiation of femininity" (Freud, 1937c, p. 250) on the part of both participants; as Freud pointed out, the treatment may then culminate in a negative therapeutic reaction or, worse, turn into an interminable analysis.

Notes

1. "If the addiction to gambling, with the unsuccessful struggles to break the habit and the opportunities it affords for self-punishment, is a repetition of the compulsion to masturbate, we shall not be surprised to find that it occupied such a large space in Dostoevsky's life. After all, we find no cases of severe neurosis in which the auto-erotic satisfaction of early childhood and of puberty has not played a part" (Freud, 1928b, p. 194).
2. Freud points out that in the novella, "the mother [is equated] with a prostitute" and that "she did not, as a mother, escape her quite unconscious transference of love on to her son" (Freud, 1928b, pp. 193–194).
3. "It is true that Zweig's story is told by the mother, not by the son. It must flatter the son to think: 'if my mother only knew what dangers masturbation involves me in, she would certainly save me from them by allowing me to lavish all my tenderness on her own body' " (Freud, 1928b, p. 193).
4. In his masterly study of Dostoevsky's heroes, V. Marinov writes: "The satyr–father of the Karamazov brothers breathes indelible sensuality into each of his sons" (Marinov, 1990).
5. The Sphinx, in fact, "consumes/consummates" and "devours" the young men she questions with her riddle. Symbol of the dangerous pregenital mother, the Sphinx may also represent a wounded and screaming maternal instinct, guilty of the most hideous of murders. It would thus represent Jocasta-as-mother, split-off from Jocasta-as-woman. In killing Laïos, Oedipus puts an end to the splitting and avenges Jocasta (since Laïos had reduced her maternal instinct to nothing). See Braunschweig & Fain (1971).
6. I borrow this expression from Jean Gillibert, whose excellent aphorism I would like to recall here: "The erotic figure of the father appears as an imaginary *locus* on a line somewhere between dividing and linking [. . .] In life and in death, the father figure alternates between ferociously erotic and tenderly protective, and between prohibiting and persecuting" (Gillibert, 1979).
7. "Chr. H. I sign a bond with this Satan, to be his bounden son, and in the ninth year to belong to him body and soul" (dated 1669) (Freud, 1923d, p. 93)
8. See de Urtubey (1983). I base my argument here on the very interesting hypothesis put forward in Chapter Fourteen of that book as to Freud's interpretative modalities concerning the devil imago in "A seventeenth-century demonological neurosis"

9. I am grateful to C. Couvreur for drawing my attention to the fact that Freud's comment on his father's death contains very similar wording to that of the "burning child" dream (which calls to mind the child in Goethe's poem—see below).
10. From *The Poems of Goethe*, translated in the original metres by Edgar Alfred Bowring, 1874.
11. An earlier translation of this section appeared under the title "The Concept of psychic homosexuality" in *The International Journal of Psycho-Analysis* (1995) *76*: 793–804.
12. In the dream, I was represented by the rickety-looking hut, the only shelter his ego and loved objects had; he was afraid that I would be unable to contain the tidal wave of his instinctual drives and to shelter him from it.
13. [Translator's note: "Padded cell" is another sense of the French word *cabanon*, which also means "hut".]
14. [Translator's note: In France, when a milk tooth falls out, it is placed under the sleeping child's pillow and, during the night, is replaced by a gift "brought by a little mouse".
15. [Translator's note: The French word *souris* means "smile" (from the verb *sourire*) as well as "mouse".]
16. [Translator's note: There is a play on words here in the French text: "AIDS" is *Sida* and "flabbergasted" is *sidéré*.]
17. I base my remarks here on comments made by André Green in a discussion with Florence Guignard on femininity and masculinity that took place in 1985 in the Paris Psychoanalytical Society (Green, 1986a).

CHAPTER SIX

"Analysis terminable and interminable"—refusing the feminine dimension

Refusing the feminine dimension

What metapsychological interpretation could nowadays be given to Freud's metaphor of the "underlying bedrock" linked to refusing the feminine dimension or, as he himself put it (Freud, 1937c, p. 250), the repudiation of femininity?

After Freud, who saw in the repudiation of femininity in both sexes a bedrock, some French psychoanalysts have made their own contribution to that interpretation. Green, for example, sees in it an expression of the horror of being made to adopt a passive position, linked in the mind to "primary maternal madness" and to the mother's femininity; the latter has to be rejected at all costs because of the fact that it tends to produce passivity (Green, 1975, p. 62; 1990, p. 186). Fain sees in it a defensive manoeuvre aimed at containing the imago of a destructive mother endowed with the power to put to death (Fain, 1987, p. 18). For Guignard (1997), rejecting the feminine dimension implies that representations of maternal sexuality have to be pushed as far as possible into the background, and, for Schaeffer (1997), repudiating the feminine sphere is an expression of the ego's resistance as regards submitting to the constant thrust of the sexual drives and thereby allowing great quantities of de-fused libidinal excitation to emerge.

In Freud's view, both the patient's ability to internalize the feminine dimension and the extent to which the latter *can* be internalized are decisive factors in assessing the patient's "analysability" and in predicting the outcome of the analysis. Psychoanalysts are particularly concerned with preventing negative transference becoming too well established in the treatment, since it can all too easily prove rebellious to any attempt at interpretation and turn into a *negative therapeutic reaction* (or, as Cournut puts it, a "negative psychoanalytic reaction" (Cournut, 1988)) that devitalizes the psychoanalytic process, fossilizes it and transforms it into a "bedrock".

To illustrate this situation—it gives the analyst an "oppressive feeling" (Freud, 1937c, p. 252)—Freud proposed three clinical examples of negative trends in "Analysis terminable and interminable". The junction common to these three heterogeneous trajectories lies at the heart of the transference neurosis, its quality and the conditions under which it can be analysed.

For Freud, each of these cases illustrates the "transference illness" that remained unresolved when negativity, related to an unanalysed—in fact almost unidentified—negative transference, re-emerged in such a way as to cause the psychoanalytic process to break down. Negativity appears in a different disguise in each case but it always relates to one of the parameters that condition what can be expected from psychoanalytic treatment (change, new openings, etc.).

It is important also to note that each of the cases Freud mentions dates from before the turning-point of 1920, i.e., before the major theoretical review that the second topographical and drive theory entailed. In chronological order, Freud reports, in "Analysis terminable and interminable", on his psychoanalytic venture with the Wolf-Man, Sandor Ferenczi, and Emma Eckstein.

The momentous analysis of the Wolf-Man, whom Freud refers to as "a young Russian", lasted from 1910 to 1914. The treatment was resumed several times, with Freud and with other analysts, after 1918. Given the complex psychic landscape of that patient and the crucial theoretical issues he raised, Freud spent a great deal of time and energy with him, both during and after the analysis itself.

Sandor Ferenczi—"who had himself practised analysis with great success", writes Freud (1937c, p. 221)—was analysed by Freud in several short phases between 1914 and 1916. Both protagonists of that analytic situation claimed that Ferenczi's analysis did indeed allow the development of a true psychoanalytic process (Freud–Ferenczi, 1914), but the very close links of friendship that already existed between the two men would tend to suggest that the thorny question of the *choice of analyst* ought to have been uppermost in their minds.

Freud's third example is the analysis of Emma Eckstein, which took place in 1895. Though short—nine months—the analysis was punctuated by unforeseen incidents. In addition, it took place at a time when Freud was discovering fantasy, the transference, and the setting, and when he was trying to establish the theory of seduction as the traumatic aetiology of hysteria—in other words, at a time when he had only just begun to lay the initial foundations of what was to develop into the practice of psychoanalysis.

For Freud, these three cases—which *a priori* had nothing in common—in fact share a common denominator: the "bedrock" that is "repudiation of femininity" (or, in more modern language, the denial of the feminine dimension). It was this that, in each of the three cases, brought negativity back into the analysis and led to failure.

Nevertheless, Freud's position invites us indirectly to ask the question: in each of the three cases, was rejection of the feminine sphere to be laid only at the *patient's* door? In other words, when negativity comes into analyses via the "bedrock" represented by "repudiation of femininity", is this not due to the fact that rejection of the feminine dimension has not been sufficiently processed in the *analyst's* countertransference, thereby creating blind spots that hinder the work of interpretation?

(A) In the Wolf-Man case, as Freud admits in "Analysis terminable and interminable", he found himself faced with a form of entropy as regards change, connected in part to the phenomenon of repetition that became established in the "young Russian's" transference psycho-neurosis: the negative therapeutic reaction has as its roots the rejection of the feminine dimension, here translated as abhorrence of adopting a passive attitude towards another man. Nevertheless, we could surmise that the violent projections Freud was subjected to from the very first session onwards may have made it difficult for him to distinguish, in the "young Russian", between what could be accounted for by the contradictions of the feminine sphere and his anal defensive organization when faced with the anxiety aroused by psychic homosexuality. Consequently, integrating certain features of his desired object was a source of many problems.

(B) Sandor Ferenczi's situation could best be described as inversely homothetic to that of the Wolf-Man, because this time it was Ferenczi who, long after his apparently successful psychoanalysis with Freud, blamed the latter for not having sufficiently analysed the negative transference—indeed for denying that it had even existed, on the grounds that it had not been obvious during the actual analysis. We shall see below that, though they use the same form of words, Freud and Ferenczi were not really referring to the same "negative transference"; for Freud, this was primarily a paternal form of the transference, whereas for Ferenczi it was mainly a regressive transference of a maternal and feminine sort, focusing on object relations. Hence, in Ferenczi's case, denial of the feminine dimension, bringing in its wake the negative transference that led to the failed analysis, can be seen as a failure to analyse his maternal transference and identifications; that failure was in part due to the fact that the male psychoanalyst found it difficult to accept this kind of transference coming from a male patient.

(C) As for Emma Eckstein, Freud's 1937 paper invites us to reflect on the confusion that existed in this patient between external and internal, and on the destiny of trauma. Here we have every reason to believe that the return of negativity, linked to rejection of the feminine sphere (in a woman, in this case), was mainly due to her hatred of her mother's feminine and maternal dimensions (Bégoin-Guignard, 1987), with that hatred being turned back on herself. Nevertheless, if we take into account Emma's analytic history, we could say also (and I shall try to prove this hypothesis below), that the destiny of the patient's trauma had its roots in something that, having remained unanalysed, returned to haunt the patient long after the analysis had ended. The origins of this unanalysed aspect probably lay in the analyst's negation of an unconscious homosexual link, a negation based on the need to obliterate his own feminine dimension and push it as far as possible into the background.

It is therefore a crucial question for the practice of psychoanalysis when the negative contradictions of certain transference patterns come up against blind spots in the analyst's countertransference relating to rejection of the feminine dimension. It may indeed be that question that Freud after all was trying to elaborate on, given his insistence, in the 1937 paper, on the importance of the analyst's personal analysis. If so, we should perhaps look upon "Analysis terminable and interminable" as a self-analytic paper and as such completely in line with "A disturbance of memory on the Acropolis" (Freud, 1936a), written the year before.

Three negative variations on a theme

(A) The "young Russian" (the Wolf-Man)

The Wolf-Man analysis represents a genuine epistemological break with the past in Freud's conception of infantile neurosis. Though we now talk of the "1920 turning point" in Freud's thinking, it seems quite obvious that the shift actually began in 1914—with all the consequences that it entailed for the rest of Freud's work—immediately after the Wolf-Man analysis and thanks to the theoretical and practical obstacles Freud had to deal with in the course of the treatment. We know that the Wolf-Man analysis demanded a great deal of Freud; indeed, it considerably unsettled him from the point of view both of theory and of the countertransference. It was hardly surprising, therefore, that this analysis in particular (Freud thought of it as a failure[1]) came into Freud's mind as an illustration of certain technical and theoretical dead-ends he was to discuss in his 1937 paper.

In "Analysis terminable and interminable", Freud points out that in the "young Russian's" analysis he was faced with a negative transference that developed into a negative therapeutic reaction. Fearing that the analysis was becoming bogged down and might therefore prove interminable—due, at least in part, to resistance based on dependence and to the force of the Wolf-Man's passivity-inducing action—Freud "resorted to the heroic measure of fixing a time-limit for the analysis" (Freud, 1937c, p. 217); this decision "must be left to the analyst's tact", since "a lion only springs once" (*ibid.*, p. 219). Freud himself admits this device meant that only limited aspects of his patient's infantile psycho-neurosis could be brought to light, and that the analysis of the transference neurosis was never really gone into, blocked as it was by the negative transference whose effects became apparent only after the main analysis had come to an end.

The analysis was resumed some five years later, at the end of 1918 or the beginning of 1919, then the patient had further analysis with Ruth Mack Brunswick. These proved necessary because "part of the transference had not been resolved"; these "residual patterns [. . .] showed a distinctly paranoid character" (*ibid.*, p. 218). In putting matters thus, Freud was in essence posing the problem, via the negative aspects, of the forces of destruction at work in repetition.

Freud quite obviously realized that the Wolf-Man's "insanity" had to do with the organization and management of his bisexuality;[2] it would seem, however, that one of the reasons that made this analysis *interminable* was Freud's apparent inability to analyse the splitting that was occurring in the transference—splitting was probably unavoidable in this case, given the patient's abhorrence of the feminine dimension and the permanent nature of its "denial", probably related to the fear of becoming insane that certain fantasies of being made passive imply—the transference thereby becoming both split-off and actively splitting.

This analysis manifestly enabled a great deal of light to be thrown on the organization of the young Russian's infantile psycho-neurosis and on the development of the obsessional neurosis based on his anal–sadistic character and anal eroticism. However, the analysis did not allow Freud to modify in depth certain pathological aspects of the Wolf-Man's states of mind—in particular those outlined in the spectacular fantasies reported in the very first session of the analysis.

Trials and tribulations

When Sergueï Constantinovitch Pankejeff consulted Freud, the "young Russian, a man spoilt by wealth [. . .] had come to Vienna in a state of complete helplessness, accompanied by a private doctor and an attendant" (*ibid.*, p. 217). This condition had lasted for the previous five years; it began after a gonorrhoeal infection had precipitated a nervous breakdown. The famous psychiatrists he consulted over the next few years (Betcherev in St Petersburg, Kraepelin in Munich, and Ziehen in Berlin) diagnosed his illness as manic-depressive insanity. From age eighteen to twenty-three, the patient went more or less from convalescent home to fashionable sanatorium, depending on the time of year and his fits of depression, undergoing various kinds of treatment (massage, hydrotherapy, etc.), which all turned out to be of little use.

In addition, he had experienced a certain number of trials and tribulations over the years since his illness began.

The first dramatic event was the suicide of his sister Anna, who was two years older than Sergueï, by mercury poisoning when she was twenty-one. Anna was one of the central figures of Sergueï's childhood: when he was just over three years of age, she had "seduced him into sexual practices" (Freud, 1918b, p. 20). A highly intelligent girl, she dominated him from many points of view and, as a result, had become her father's favourite; in the past, the family used to say that Sergueï ought to have been the girl and his sister the boy. This had contributed to the fact that Sergueï felt very disappointed, jealous and angry.

The second dramatic event was the father's suicide, two years after that of Anna, in 1908. A rich landowner, treated over many a long year for manic-depressive illness—he was hospitalized in a psychiatric clinic for the first time when Sergueï was six—he probably committed suicide by taking an overdose of veronal. The mother, described as being quite a cold and unfriendly person, was hypochondriac and not very good at looking after her children. When Sergueï was a boy, she was always concerned about her own misfortunes and hardly stopped complaining that she "could not go on living like this". She taught him biblical stories at the time when he was feeling particularly anxious, around age 4½, in the hope of making him less irritable and less anxious. This was the beginning of an obsessional neurotic front that gradually became more and more extensive, persisting until Sergueï was over ten years old. After his father's death, the inheritance was shared out between Sergueï and his mother; she administered his fortune. Though he admitted she did this in a wholly disinterested manner, and indeed that she was extremely generous towards him, Sergueï nevertheless sharply criticized the fact that he depended on her financially.

In 1908, he met Thérèse, an extremely beautiful nurse, in a sanatorium near Munich that Kraepelin had recommended to him. Thérèse was older than Sergueï, she was divorced, and had a little girl. He had hardly set eyes on her at a ball when he fell in love with her and determined to make her his mistress. Their affair was a tumultuous one, mainly because of the young Russian's changeable and contradictory feelings towards her; she, for her part, hoped that he would soon propose to her. Faced with the idea of having to commit himself more deeply, the Wolf-Man, after much procrastination, decided to break off the affair once and for all. Hardly had they broken up but once again he fell into a depressive state that left him unable to take any decision or any action.

On his mother's advice, he consulted in Odessa, some time in 1909, a young psychiatrist named Drosnes[3] who, having read Freud, told Sergueï about psychoanalysis and offered him "psychotherapy". However, after a few months, Drosnes had to face the facts: with no personal experience of analysis and lacking the necessary equipment for bringing the proposed treatment to a successful conclusion, he gave up. A trip to Vienna was thereupon arranged and, after his first meeting with Freud, the extremely wealthy young Russian began the analysis that was later to make him famous. The least that can be said is that this analysis did not begin in an innocuous fashion . . .

The first session

Thanks to a letter Freud wrote to Sandor Ferenczi on 13 February 1910, we know the general content of the Wolf-Man's first session: "A wealthy young Russian, whom I am treating for compulsive and passionate feelings of love, confessed to me, after the first session, the following transferences: Jewish swindler, he would like to use me from behind and shit on my head." Freud goes on to write that, when the patient was six years old, the first manifest symptom consisted in blasphemous insults directed at God: swine, dog, etc. Whenever he saw three heaps of horse-dung in the street, he felt anxious because of the Holy Trinity and he would look anxiously around for a fourth one in order to chase away this thought.[4] (Freud & Ferenczi, 1994).

What a surprise this must have been for Freud! We can well imagine how puzzled he felt on hearing these fantasies, and we can easily understand that, when such raw and overwhelming fantasies suddenly emerged in the way they did, he judged it necessary to place an intermediary between himself and his young patient in the person of Ferenczi and the correspondence they were exchanging. What undoubtedly motivated Freud's wish to discuss the matter with Ferenczi was the instantaneous enactment represented by the sudden appearance and abrupt evacuation of a homosexual and scatological scenario concerning Freud himself.

In this first session, a jumble of fantasy productions emerged that from then on were to weave the basic outline of Sergueï Pankejeff's analysis. Even though our own experience teaches us that very often the first session of an analysis contains the themes and material that are destined to play a major role for several years to come, we feel nevertheless somewhat astonished at the sight of the material, in condensed form and expressed in a very particular fashion, that the young Russian reported in this first session. It is impossible not to think that a major part of the future development of the Wolf-Man's analysis is contained in the series of statements Freud makes in his letter to Ferenczi, even going so far as to speak of his patient's "transferences".

We could suggest that the text of this first session resembles the reactivated form of the fantasy situation expressed by the nightmare the patient had shortly before his fourth birthday: "five or six wolves sitting quite still on a tree". In his analysis of the wolf dream, Freud was to reconstruct the premises of this strange and violent expression of a wish relating to Sergueï Pankejeff's repressed homosexual fantasy: being copulated with by the father (Freud, 1918b).

As is well known, it was the young Russian's analysis that enabled Freud to take stock fully of the crucial role played by primal scene fantasies in structuring the psyche.

In my opinion, all the same, the scenario proposed in the Wolf-Man's first session is not a primal scene in the narrow sense of the term; it is more a paradoxical defence against invasion by traumatic affects relating to a primal scene fantasy. At first, this scenario proved impossible for both protagonists to work through in the psychoanalytic situation. It represents a homosexual type of relationship, infused with anality and the threat of castration; it expresses the quantitative torrent of energy in which Sergueï Pankejeff's mind was caught up at the beginning of the analysis, a torrent that obviously involved repetition in the psychoanalytic situation of a trauma we could suppose resembled the one which had aroused so much anxiety in him as a child on awakening from his nightmare.

Confronted with the internal chaos generated by the excitation that his fragile internal objects were unable to deal with given the pressures attaching to his mental condition, Sergueï Pankejeff immediately reproduced this scene in the transference, evacuating in his very first session a complex scenario—verbally acted out—that highlights the pathological nature of his infantile sexual theories.

I have the impression that the scenario Sergueï Pankejeff proposed to Freud is a condensation of fantasies of seduction, of castration, and of the primal scene; it is in fact a fantasy of primary narcissistic seduction, marking with its seal the failure of a genuine attempt at working through primal fantasies in order to make them meaningful. Given that he was only just beginning analysis, the young Russian was naturally enough still unable to process his affects and transference feelings; they were expressed as an insufficiently contained thrust of the instinctual drives, that was not correctly relayed by representation or metaphor—in passing too directly through the Preconscious, it posed the problem of how to qualify the mental space defined by the psychoanalytic situation. The narcissistic distress of the young Russian, "precipitated" as it were into the analytic situation and overwhelmed by unintegrated primary fantasies, led him to "pass" this scene, just as in the past, when he was eighteen months old and excited by his parents' sexual intercourse, he had "passed" a stool in order to "interrupt" it.

Thus, as we have seen, the backdrop to Sergueï Pankejeff's transference fantasy consisted of a number of elements (fictional or real) that marked his childhood and organized his infantile neurosis, as they appeared in the course of his analysis with Freud:

- "climbing" on to the Professor as the wolves in the story "climbed upon one another" and the wolves in the dream climbed into the tree (Freud, 1918b, p. 31);
- being in a position of active seduction as his sister had been with him and therefore repeating, with the Professor, her act of seduction. Freud notes:

> His sister had taken hold of his penis and played with it, at the same time telling him incomprehensible stories about his Nanya [. . .] His Nanya, she said, used to do the same thing with all kinds of people—for instance, with the gardener: she used to stand him on his head, and then take hold of his genitals. [*ibid.*, p. 20];

- given his confused identification, for Sergueï Pankejeff being "active" and "masculine" referred to his sister's masculine and Oedipal drive movements that could offer some support to his own masculine tendencies;
- "showing his bottom" to the Professor–father implied the proposal that his father penetrate him and have sexual pleasure with him; unconsciously identifying with a pregenital female figure, he would thus be able to obtain from the father a "gift–child–faeces";
- at the same time, he immediately repeated, with Freud, a clyster-type transference: the young Russian who had no "spontaneous evacuations [. . .] for months at a time" and who "had become accustomed to enemas, which were given him by an attendant" (*ibid.*, p. 74), was displaying in his very first session his constipation/enema/evacuation-of-faeces scenario;[4]
- finally, defecating on the Professor's head is a reminder of the stool he passed when he was eighteen months old, excited by parental intercourse; it is also the expression of an upheaval probably related to what he felt when his sister was seducing him—she had spoken of Nanya standing the gardener . . . on his head!

Thus the fantasy of defecating on Freud's head condenses two memories from the Wolf-Man's early childhood without transforming them hardly at all. This "reverses"—stands on its head—the

Wolf-Man's body schemata, which henceforth is "upside-down" and "back-to-front".

It is now easier to grasp the ambiguity of the anal eroticism lying behind the young Russian's identifications: passing a stool—defecating on Freud's head—is part of anal pleasure and is the anal equivalent both of a passive feminine and maternal position (receiving a baby) and of ejaculating the father's sperm (making a baby). It may also represent Sergueï Pankejeff's aggressiveness and anal sadism: "that's what my father does with my mother" in the primitive anal-sadistic version of parental sexual intercourse that later produces the birth of a new baby (Freud, 1905d).

If we analyse the scenario Sergueï Pankejeff proposes to Freud—a fantasy of homosexual penetration and seduction—we see that it contains not only the young Russian's wish to penetrate Freud but also the (obvious) wish to be penetrated by him. Faced with this wish and the intolerable castration anxiety it arouses, the Wolf-Man reverses the wish into its opposite and regresses towards an anal scenario from which emerges the desire to defecate on Freud's head, both as an act of love and as a retaliatory measure.

Unconsciously experiencing thoughts and faeces as equivalent, Sergueï Pankejeff is afraid both of the excitation relating to his wish to be penetrated by Freud and of the danger of being filled by what he feels are "thought-faeces" coming from Freud. That is why—the head being the seat of thinking—he makes a retaliatory attack with his faeces on Freud's head and thoughts. This fantasy scenario thus enables the Wolf-Man to present Freud with an eroticized representation of his desire to be mentally penetrated by him and, at the same time, of his fears that he will be dispossessed of his thoughts.

Freud's attempts at linking

Freud no doubt felt the young Russian's attack on his thinking. He immediately began to work on creating links, work which was both crucial for and beneficial to the mental distress his patient was expressing.

Refusing to let himself be disconcerted by Sergueï Pankejeff's strange and even insane transference thoughts, Freud shows in his letter to Ferenczi how these are related to the obsessional neurotic symptoms of the young Russian that appeared when he was 4½ years old.

The theory of obsessional neurosis to which Freud implicitly refers in his exchange of correspondence enables him to contain in the countertransference the brutal invasion of the (traumatic) scenario of anal penetration and defecation the young Russian expresses.

Each of the elements Freud notes ("six years old", "blasphemous insults against God", "swine", "dog", "three heaps of horse-dung", "the Holy Trinity", etc.) enables him to relate the obsessional manifestations of the Wolf-Man's childhood to the ambivalent conflict that had religion as its backdrop and cornerstone, with the two contradictory drive impulses of love and hostility towards God-the-father, i.e. towards his own father.

Taking these as his basis, Freud links the dissolution of the Oedipus complex ("six years old") with, on the one hand, death-wishes aimed at the father ("blasphemous insults against God") and, on the other, the ensuing guilt-feelings as expressed in the obsessive ritual ("three heaps of horse-dung, the Holy Trinity, searching for a fourth in order to chase away that thought").

In connecting the "Jewish swindler" with the "blasphemous insults against God: swine, dog, etc." Freud shows how the material explicitly involves the paternal transference. He is not yet ready to hear in the insult addressed to him the transference element that comes from Sergueï's conflict with his sister Anna—as a child, he feared that she might dispossess him of their father's love and, later, of their father's wealth. Behind this insult, there are probably the violent reproaches aimed at his mother—that she thought only of economizing "at his expense, and that she would probably rather see him dead so as to have sole control over the money" (Freud, 1918b, pp. 73–74).

Also, if "dog" is an obvious reference to the wolves in the nightmare (and therefore to the parents of the primal scene), "swine" recalls the association he makes later in the analysis to his sister. When as a child

> he heard that Christ had once cast out some evil spirits into a herd of swine which then rushed down a precipice, he thought of how his sister in the earliest years of her childhood, before he could

> remember, had rolled down on to a beach from the cliff-path above the harbour. She too was an evil spirit and a swine. It was a short road from here to "God-swine". His father himself had shown that he was no less of a slave to sensuality. [*ibid.*, pp. 67–68]

Similarly, in the course of the analysis, we learn that the obsessive thoughts that obliged the young Russian

> to connect God with faeces [. . .] were in fact true compromise-products, in which a part was played no less by an affectionate current of devotion than by a hostile current of abuse. "God-shit" was probably an abbreviation for an offering that one occasionally hears mentioned in its unabbreviated form. "Shitting on God" ("*auf Gott scheissen*") or "shitting something for God" ("*Gott etwas scheissen*") also means giving him a baby or getting him to give one a baby. [*ibid.*, p. 83]

In this manner, the "blasphemous insults against God" and the thoughts they brought in their wake ("three heaps of horse-dung, the Holy Trinity, the search for a fourth in order to chase away the thought") illustrate Sergueï Pankejeff's infantile omnipotence. This is projected on to God who, like the shitty and swinish Holy Trinity, represents both the combined parents in the primal scene and his sister, who nourished his own sexual curiosity.

If we look at the young Russian's family romance, a further line of interpretation can be followed. When he was a child, the family were four in number: his father, mother, sister Anna and himself. When he comes upon the *three* "heaps of horse-dung", he thinks compulsively of the "Holy Trinity", in other words of his family as it was before his own conception and birth—and this too, by contiguity, brings him closer and closer to the primal scene and the sexual play with his sister. These instinctual drive situations are intolerable to his narcissism and immediately generate destructive wishes with regard to sexuality.

Faced with the failure to suppress excitation, he sets himself up, via splitting and infantile omnipotence, as the absolute superego censor: the fourth element. The idea that the patient would anxiously search out a fourth element in order to chase away the thought therefore implies: "I am succeeding, by my very presence, in preventing them from doing those swinish and swindler-like things that fascinate me . . .".

When anality comes to the rescue of deficiencies in the feminine dimension

Even though the rest of the treatment was to confirm beyond doubt that the development of the young Russian's obsessional neurosis was based on his anal-sadistic personality and anal eroticism, we know that the analysis in itself did not enable Freud to account for the other pathological aspects of the Wolf-Man's states of mind, aspects which could be more or less expected, given the spectacular fantasies reported at the beginning of the analysis.

As I emphasized above, the fantasies expressed in Sergueï Pankejeff's first session—his first confrontation with the psychoanalytic situation—bear witness both to his finding it hard to cope and to his anxiety of traumatic origin. Though this echoed the anxiety he experienced when he awoke from his nightmare at four years of age, the need he felt to enact it verbally in the way he did does make us wonder about the sheer intensity of the experience. Why was there so much drive energy behind his need to evacuate?

The Wolf-Man's brutally defensive attitude seems all the more crucial in that it helped him to screen—and perhaps even to conceal—two problems:

- the deficiencies in his capacity for integration and working through, detrimental to his sense of identity and thought processes;
- above all, the fact that the feminine dimension, insufficiently internalized and fused with other aspects of his bisexuality, was, as a result, only partially contained.

Deficiencies in his capacity for integration and working through can be accounted for by weakness in symbol-formation. They could be due to the traumatic experiences the young Russian had in his early childhood (Freud speaks of a serious illness, perhaps pneumonia, at age three months, followed by a period of anorexia, then malaria at eighteen months of age, etc. (Freud, 1918b, pp. 37 & 98; Blum, 1974). When traumatic experiences early in life invade the mind, they facilitate the establishment of a maternal imago that arouses anxiety and perhaps even feelings of persecution, because of the fact that the baby projects on to the mother figure his or her insufficiently-contained internal drive excitation and the inchoate conflicts they give rise to. The overwhelming mental distress that results is added to the effects of the original trauma. This is one way in which the imago of a phallic pregenital mother can arise. Experienced quite literally as a foreign body that knows no bounds—and therefore as terrifyingly persecutory—this imago poses an even greater threat to the ego in that it is insufficiently contained by the paternal imago (which itself is built on shaky foundations).

The Wolf-Man's homosexual fantasies, with the explosive discharge and intensity of drive energy expressed in the first session, appear therefore to relate mainly to the need to fight against being overwhelmed by the threatening and persecutory imago of a phallic mother, an imago that in addition greatly complicated the destiny of his early identifications, both feminine and masculine.

In attempting to cope with the psychoanalytic process and the transference, the young Russian sought above all to protect his feminine dimension, insufficiently internalized and integrated with his bisexuality, through a quasi-mimetic identification (via identification with the aggressor) with a penetrating phallic–anal mother figure that aroused considerable anxiety in him. Paradoxically, Sergueï Pankejeff identified with her and her anal phallus (by definition, a "not-penis" and "not-sexualized" phallus) in order both to contain in and to expel from his mind the imago of a phallic mother. This phallic anality created gender confusion in him that, on the one hand, masked any sexual element (because of his fear of the feminine dimension) and, on the other, abolished any difference between sexes and generations (through his inability to differentiate).

This situation is far removed from that of the male homosexual wish to be anally penetrated by a penis; on the contrary, the whole point of these fantasies, which have an excremental fantasy as backdrop, is to cancel out any potential recognition of masculine and feminine—activity/passivity, part/whole, container/contained, control/letting go, etc.

It is therefore hardly surprising that one of the crucial problem situations encountered by the Wolf-Man derived from the dead-end he found himself in as a result of his negative (or inverted) Oedipus complex, with its castration complex and related underlying identifications. Castration by the father–dog–swine–wolf or by the mother–bitch–sow–she-wolf? Identification with the castrated–phallic father–wolf or with the phallic–castrated mother–she-wolf? His anger at being excluded from parental ecstasy in the primal scene kept the undecidable factor alive (this undecidable element, the "third psychic current" is the product of "bi-logical" functioning in which "yes" and "no" simultaneously exist (Green, 1990, pp. 161–164, 1993a). Caught between his resentment at not being able to experience the passionate ecstasy of his mother (via her vagina) and his anxiety at not being able to experience the passionate ecstasy of his father (via his penis), Sergueï Pankejeff developed persistent rectal and anal fixations that acted as a fulcrum for potentiating and representing his erotic insanity, the "compulsive falling in love" (Freud, 1918b, p. 117).

This factor meant that it was difficult for Freud to distinguish clearly between what, in the "young Russian" was due to the contradictions within his feminine dimension and what constituted a defensive anal organization against homosexuality.

It is undeniable that Sergueï Pankejeff's alienated transference, marking the non-neurotic character of his mental functioning, put Freud's countertransference to a severe test. Linked to an element of pathological splitting in the transference, the resultant unanalysability of the situation was expressed as a highly active negative transference that silently went on to generate a significant negative therapeutic reaction.

As regards this first session, it would seem that the persistence of the negative transference and its development into a negative therapeutic reaction—expressed as the Wolf-Man's subsequent submissiveness after the interruption imposed by Freud (and experienced by the patient as his not having any choice in the matter)—were perhaps due to the fact that Freud was unable to allow Sergueï Pankejeff to think through the characteristics of his desired object as projected on to the analyst in that session. This inability of Freud's may therefore have enabled the Wolf-Man to fulfil the inaugural fantasy of his analysis—the fantasy of evacuating Freud, the attempt in other words to bring the whole analysis down to a clyster when faced with the anxiety and horror generated by fantasies in which he would be made passive, one expression of his rejection of the feminine dimension.

(B) "A certain man, who had himself practised analysis with great success . . ." (Sandor Ferenczi)

As for Ferenczi, the problem of the backlash effect of the negative transference was expressed in a perspective I call inversely homothetic to that of the young Russian: it was Ferenczi himself who, long after the apparent success of his analysis, reproached Freud with having failed to analyse the negative transference properly (in other words, with having "denied" the negative transference by failing to acknowlegde it as such). As a result, Ferenczi had been unable to regress further and therefore benefit from a much more in-depth analysis.

We now know, thanks to their published correspondence, what kind of difficulty the two protagonists of that analytic situation had to confront. Without going into detail, I would remind the reader that Freud agreed to analyse Ferenczi—somewhat unwillingly, it must be said, given that he had already postponed the undertaking on several occasions—as a result of the upheavals of the First World War. The analysis took place between 1914 and 1916 in three phases, each of which lasted three weeks. Both Ferenczi and Freud were later to acknowledge that the analysis had had some positive results, but it is clear today that Ferenczi never at any time felt he had been able to obtain the kind of benefit he had hoped for (Ferenczi, 1932).

The *Correspondence* gives the impression that the analysis was broken off, before reaching any real conclusion, just as Ferenczi was trying to deal with his maternal transference; this seems hardly to have been analysed at all, mainly because of Freud's reluctance to accept this aspect of Ferenczi's transference.[5]

Ferenczi's feelings of hate towards Freud

Let us return to Ferenczi's reproaching Freud for not analysing the negative transference, the source, he argued, of subsequent difficulties in his own practice as analyst. These reproaches are stated unambiguously in a letter he wrote to Freud on 17 January 1930, in which Ferenczi claims that, in their relationship, there was—at least from Ferenczi's point of view—a mixture of different conflicting emotions and positions. At first Freud represented a revered teacher and unattainable model, with Ferenczi very much in the position of pupil—and such feelings are inevitably mixed. Freud then became Ferenczi's analyst, but, says the latter, unfavourable circumstances prevented that analysis from going as far as it might have. Ferenczi particularly regretted the fact that Freud did not perceive his analysand's negative feelings and fantasies, partly transferred, and thus allow them to be abreacted. Even the most experienced of practitioners, adds Ferenczi, requires help in this; as a result, he was forced to undertake a methodical self-analysis that he found quite distressing.

In his reply, dated 20 January 1930, Freud wrote that he had been amused by certain passages, especially those in which Ferenczi had complained that Freud had not analysed the negative transference. In his reproaches, Freud continued, Ferenczi seemed to have forgotten the fact that at that time nobody—including Freud himself—realized with any degree of certainty that negative transference and negative reactions were to be expected in every case. Anyway, he added, given the excellent relationship they had, it would have taken some considerable time for it to become manifest.[6]

At this crucial point in his relationship with Freud, Ferenczi seems rather obviously to be confirming what he had written some eight years previously in a letter to Groddeck dated 27 February 1922. In that letter, Ferenczi says that "Professor Freud" spent an hour or so dealing with his (Ferenczi's) condition; Freud was still of the opinion he had expressed before, namely that the principal feature had to do with Ferenczi's feelings of hate towards him, given that Freud (like the father before him) had prevented Ferenczi from marrying a younger woman (the daughter of the woman he did in fact marry). This factor engendered in Ferenczi murderous feelings towards Freud, as expressed in scenes of nocturnal death (growing cold, moaning). These symptoms, adds Ferenczi, appear over-determined by reminiscences of witnessing parental intercourse. He goes on to say that he felt better after talking, for once, about the animosity towards the father he adored (Ferenczi & Groddeck, 2002).

Two types of negative transference

How then are we to understand the justification for Ferenczi's complaint, in 1930, that the negative transference had not been analysed and worked through to its conclusion? How are we to understand the fact that Ferenczi suspected Freud of neither recognizing nor properly assessing the secret power of that kind of transference in the course of Ferenczi's analysis—and perhaps of having had a negative countertransference reaction (or even a negative psychoanalytic reaction) towards him?

Are we to take it to be a simple loss of memory on his part? Or a more extreme form of repression based on a "bedrock" of negativity? A form of splitting? If this were indeed the case, what would be the effect of the destiny of the transference neurosis which at that moment gave rise to such apparently unjustified complaints? What would be the status of the residual hatred that at the time had remained in the dark, only to emerge several years later?

In fact there would seem to be neither contradiction nor paradox in these different parameters. If we follow closely Ferenczi's thinking and his technical and theoretical work in the ten years from 1920 to 1930, one thing becomes immediately obvious to today's reader: the negative transference of which Freud speaks is of a different category from that of Ferenczi. What Freud calls negative transference develops through the vicissitudes of an essentially *paternal* transference situation, whereas for Ferenczi the negative transference of which he was speaking at that time implies a *maternal and feminine* type of transference focusing on identification with the mother and on the primary relationship with the object (Bokanowski, 1994). The fact that the same term was employed at that period to describe both types of transference and that Freud apparently did not feel any need to give a more precise definition—this illustrates his difficulty with respect to being the mother-figure in the transference—inevitably gave rise to conceptual vagueness and contributed to maintaining a state of confusion between the two men. It therefore becomes easier to understand how the "bedrock" of "repudiation of femininity" (denial of the feminine dimension) had this backlash effect, given the analyst's avoidance of being in the position of a maternal and feminine transference object.

(C) "An unmarried woman, no longer young . . ." (Emma Eckstein)

It is interesting to note that what Freud has to say about Emma

Eckstein in "Analysis terminable and interminable" follows directly on, as a kind of association, from his account of the psychoanalytic relationship he had with Ferenczi: "I now pass on to my second example, which raises the same problem" (Freud, 1937c, p. 222). It would therefore be legitimate to think that this new example, concerning as it does a woman, represents in Freud's mind a complementary aspect of the maternal transference that he had just mentioned in connection with Ferenczi.

Before we consider Freud's report on his psychoanalytic relationship with Emma Eckstein in "Analysis terminable and interminable", let me digress a little. It is thanks to Anzieu (1959) and to Masson (1985) that we are able to identify the woman patient Freud speaks of in his 1937 paper. Anzieu adds that Emma Eckstein is one of the people on whom is based the probably "composite" image of "Irma", the principal character in the dream known as "Irma's injection", the centrepiece dream of *Die Traumdeutung* (Freud, 1900a).

A virgin, sacrificed and bloody . . .

Let me briefly remind the reader of what we know today of this young woman's psychoanalytic history with Freud. He treated her for hysterical symptoms in 1895 (since puberty, she had found it almost impossible to walk, she suffered from stomach pains and dysmenorrhoea, attributed by Freud to intense masturbatory activity); on Freud's advice, she underwent an operation on her turbinate bones, with Fliess as surgeon. The operation was a disaster: Fliess forgot to remove a two-foot length of iodoform gauze from one of the turbinate bones, which led to suppuration and nasal haemorrhage. When it was removed some weeks later by a different surgeon, another massive haemorrhage ensued, bringing about a state of shock and causing severe physical sequellae—she remained disfigured, a factor which contributed to restricting her hopes of falling in love and marrying (Anzieu, 1959). Since, among other things, Fliess refused to acknowledge his error, this affair weighed heavily on the relationship between him and Freud: the "Irma's injection" dream is in part related to Freud's need to clear his own name as well as to block any further doubts that were growing about his friend Fliess's professional standing and moral probity, the aim being to try to keep Fliess as a friend (Freud needed his friendship at that point).

As Anzieu points out, Emma was a virgin, sacrificed and bloody, on the altar of the chaste homosexual love between Freud and Fliess. We could indeed consider Emma as an image, for both men, of the "hole" represented by the enigma of femininity and the feminine dimension (the "dark continent" (Freud, 1926e, p. 212)); they explored this *locus* thanks to the pact of denial they established together, a pact which was both "negation of desire and denial of the homosexual link between them based on erasing the unknown aspect of femininity" (Kaës, 1989, p. 110).

Again, we learn from a letter written to Fliess by Freud on 12 December 1897 that less than two years after ending the analysis with Emma (Irma), Freud referred a woman patient to her for therapy. According to Anzieu, she would therefore have been the first person after Freud to practise psychoanalysis. Emma remained active until she was forty. After her two elder sisters married, she kept house for her mother. In 1905, probably at the approach of menopause but also after some setbacks in her financial situation, the break-up of a love affair and the abandonment of all hope of marriage, she had a relapse: genital haemorrhages re-appeared and she again became unable to walk. She was confined to bed, withdrew from worldly affairs and surrounded herself with books; she suffered from an inexplicable illness that her family called hysterical and she thought was purely physical. Instead of resuming her analysis, she preferred to undergo an operation on a myoma; Freud disapproved of this operation, which was accompanied by a complete hysterectomy. She fell in love with the surgeon, hid her romantic ideas and wallowed in masochistic daydreams about fearful changes to the inside of her body; she complained to Freud, who, says Anzieu, indignantly refused to grant her a resumption of her analysis, abandoning her to her neurosis until she died in 1924. Freud steadfastly maintained that, but for the new trauma, there would have been no fresh outbreak of her neurosis (Anzieu, 1959[1988, pp. 185–186]).

This information completes that given in Freud's "Analysis terminable and interminable". There, Freud tells us he treated the young woman for "three-quarters of a year" for a hysterical paralysis of her legs. "In the years following her recovery, she was consistently unfortunate" (1937c, p. 222). She was a support to her family in times of need, but remained unmarried. Fifteen years after her analysis, she developed a myoma which required a complete hysterectomy. After that operation, she became ill once more, developed erotomaniac fantasies involving the surgeon and, as Freud puts it, "proved inaccessible to a further attempt at analysis" (*ibid.*).

An imaginary child

Let us try to follow Freud's account of Emma's analysis, keeping in mind the other information in our possession.

Since puberty, this young woman suffered from an inability to walk, owing to severe pains in her legs. This hysterical condition had defied all kinds of treatment, but was removed thanks to a nine-month-long analysis (the normal length of time for a pregnancy . . .); we could surmise that Emma needed this length of time to exchange the expression of a defensive wish for a penis (the paralysis) for the acknowledgement of her wish to obtain a child from the father (here, in the transference, Freud).

Later, certain events concerning her family—Freud calls them "disasters" (1937c, p. 222)—convinced both patient and analyst that, as a result, "every hope of happiness in love and marriage (vanished)" (*ibid.*). We may well think that external reality was here functioning as a blind spot in the analyst's countertransference, with the probable aim

- on the one hand, of no longer having to think that perhaps Fliess's operation, with its physical sequellae that disfigured Emma, was the true cause of the disappearance of her hopes of happiness;
- on the other, of concealing from himself the fact that nothing had changed in Emma's Oedipal cathexes, even though she was by now a woman who "stood up to all this valiantly and was a support to her family in difficult times" (*ibid.*).

Some twelve to fourteen years after her first analysis (and the operation carried out by Fliess), she suffered from profuse haemorrhages due to a myoma, and this necessitated a complete hysterectomy (i.e., another operation). Perhaps the age at which Emma presented this myoma corresponded to the age at which her mother became pregnant with her . . . Another possibility: the age at which Emma had to accept the idea that she would never herself become a mother one day. Freud's account gives no further information on this point. What we can imagine, however, is that twelve or fourteen years after the initial analysis—i.e., the age at which the imaginary child (Stein, 1971) whom she desired to have with Freud in the transference would reach puberty—the patient developed a symptom that affected her body quite differently, more involved with her feminine identity (as woman and mother) than was the phallic pathology of paralysis of and severe pains in her legs. This new symptom, though less symbolic in its expression, had a more destructive impact and echoed in a pathological way the primal fantasies that lay behind Emma's Oedipal organization.

Freud says that from the time of this operation, she became ill once more, and developed erotomania (a passionate transference) with respect to the surgeon. This was obviously a displacement on to the surgeon of the transference love and hate that had not been resolved in the analysis with Freud. Yet the question remains as to what kind of transference love and hate was involved in this case: paternal and/or maternal?

"Fearful changes in her inside . . ."

If we continue reading Freud's 1937 paper, we see that in addition to her erotomania (the expression of unresolved transference love and hate), Emma had "masochistic phantasies about the fearful changes in her inside—phantasies with which she concealed her romance" (1937c, p. 222). These "fearful changes in her inside" echo what Klein wrote of the young girl's fantasies as the Oedipal situation develops, revolving around her identificatory rivalry with the object (the mother) of a double desire, one which is both primary and secondarily homosexual (Klein, 1932). In other words, the feeling is that the transformations taking place inside the body are expressions of instinctual drive impulses involving unanalysed hatred—turned back against her own self—of her mother's feminine and maternal dimensions.

According to Freud, the myoma—from which Emma would die—"may have been a different manifestation of the same repressed impulses" (*ibid.*), in other words, those that had not been taken up in the transference with him as an object to be analysed during those initial nine months, and which gave rise to a fresh outbreak almost fifteen years later—this time in negative form, leading to defusion and destruction, to castration . . . and, ultimately, to death. Thus, Emma's negative maternal transference, given the unanalysed hatred she, as a woman in analysis with a man, felt towards her feminine and maternal dimensions, led, in the end, to an unresolved "transference illness". The "bedrock" of "repudiation of femininity" (rejection of the feminine dimension) that produces the backlash effect of the negative transference (in this case, in a woman) would appear to involve hatred of her mother's feminine and maternal dimensions; the failure to express this hatred in the transference at the time of her initial analysis meant that, much later, it reverted against her own self—just when she had to prepare for the fact that she would never herself be a mother.

The homosexual alliance and rejection of the feminine dimension

Nevertheless, given what we now know of Emma's history, we would have some justification in suggesting that the "destiny" of Emma's trauma had its roots in the homosexual alliance between Freud and Fliess. Though they "denied" any such alliance, it was probably based (as I have suggested) on their efforts to erase or to put to one side their own feminine aspects (projected, at that moment in time, on to Emma), because of the anxiety each of them felt when faced with the *unknown* character of these aspects.

The unanalysed components of that situation rebounded many years later via Emma's passionate transference towards the surgeon who practised the hysterectomy; by displacement, he condensed both the Freud–Fliess couple that had decided on the mucous membrane of the nose/uterus operation, and the surgeon whom Freud had called in after Fliess's initial operation.

It would seem, therefore, that contradictions in an unanalysed negative transference emerge when denial of the feminine dimension constitutes a blind spot in the analyst's countertransference (a blind spot created by the unconscious homosexual relationship—psychic homosexuality—between Freud and Fliess). As a result, the analyst can no longer put himself into a feminine and maternal position in the transference, the only position that would allow for proper interpretation of his female patient's impulses of rivalry and hatred (concerning the feminine and maternal dimensions) towards her own mother.

To return to the suggestion I made above, the case of Emma Eckstein, as a "free association" that came to Freud while he was writing his 1937 paper, illustrates a complementary aspect of the problem of the feminine and maternal transference raised by Ferenczi in his psychoanalytic relationship with Freud; we can now see *two* possible paths by which the "bedrock" of "repudiation of femininity" can emerge as a resistance in the analyst's countertransference and set a limit to analysis. In Ferenczi's case, the feminine dimension in a man being analysed by another man generates, in the analyst, certain countertransference resistances against analysing the maternal component. In Emma Eckstein's case, the problem is that of the feminine dimension in a woman analysed by a man who had repressed his own feminine component, thereby creating in himself a blind spot as regards the hatred his woman patient feels for the maternal dimension.

Notes

1. "This being beaten is now a convergence of the sense of guilt and sexual love. *It is not only the punishment for the forbidden genital relation, but also the regressive substitute for that relation . . .*" (Freud, 1919e, p. 189, original italics).
2.. Green (1990) highlights the contrast between Freud's perspicacity and analytic shrewdness on the one hand, and the flimsiness, not to say insufficiency, of the results obtained
3. As Green (1990) notes, when the young Russian wonders whether the wolves were male or female, the answer was "at this time the question was not yet settled" (Freud, 1918b, p. 25).
4. Leonid Drosnes was one of the first Russian psychoanalysts. He was elected a member of the Viennese Association in January 1911; later, he practised psychoanalysis in St Petersburg.
5. Letter 112F. Freud had already mentioned to Ferenczi, in a letter dated 8 February 1910 (110F), that he had taken on a new patient from

Odessa, whom he described as a very wealthy Russian suffering from "compulsive feelings".

6. Freud writes in his case report: "At last I recognized the importance of the intestinal trouble for my purposes: it represented the small trait of hysteria which is regularly to be found at the root of an obsessional neurosis" (Freud 1918b (1914): 75].

The reader may wish to refer, in particular, to Letter 603F, dated 24 March 1916, in which Freud writes that what he found surprising was the sheer number of devices that Ferenczi put into operation as he came close to fulfilling his repressed wish to master the maternal figure in any shape or form. Freud admits that he had underestimated the strength of this complex, no doubt through lack of personal experience.

The reader will have noticed that the arguments Freud put forward in his 1930 letter concerning the absence of any negative transference in Ferenczi are exactly the same as those he used in "Analysis terminable and interminable" (Freud, 1937c). In this paper Freud continued to justify his position: ". . . not every good relation between an analyst and his subject during and after analysis was to be regarded as a transference" (*ibid.*, p. 222). Later in the same paper (p. 231), Freud says that the "warning that we should let sleeping dogs lie [. . .] is peculiarly inapposite when applied to the conditions of mental life"; if the dogs are really sleeping "it is not in our power to awaken them"—in other words, to arouse a negative transference where there are no visible or ostensible signs of it.

Conclusion

Psyche—movement and change in the mind

Since any true description of the practice of psychoanalysis must have as its foundation the mental work done by both participants in the psychoanalytic situation, a definition of psyche would seem to be contingent on the relationship between the two minds in presence.

Psyche is both transformation and a reflection of the complexities of transformation.

Since psychoanalysis leaves its mark on a whole series of processes and can produce an infinite set of modifications, it also, like psyche, opens on to transformation and reflects similar complexities. To that extent, analysis is a paradigm of mental life.

Maurice Blanchot seems to be emphasizing the "im-pressive" aspect of psychoanalysis when he says it is characterized by the fact that it constitutes "a movement whose term is unpredictable and whose conclusion brings in its wake, like a new propensity, the impossibility of conclusion"; its finality is "to be always finite and infinite, terminable and interminable in Freud's words. When it begins, it begins without end" (Blanchot, 1969, p. 353).

If we adopt that point of view, we could see in the polysemous title of "Analysis terminable and interminable" a reflection of the idea that the *psyche* itself is interminable.

Mental processes, intrinsically dependent on states of mind at the same time as they organize these, decide what kind of change takes place throughout the course of an analysis: they lie at the heart of the psychoanalytic process, of its temporality and of its finality.

Closely related to the development of working-through and integration in the mind, the psychic movements analysis sets in motion and the changes these bring about centre on two correlated but distinct aspects of the psychoanalytic process, each of which influences that process in its own way. It is therefore necessary to begin by differentiating them.

When we speak of movement in psychoanalysis, we are attempting to represent the mind's activity *per se*; the mind is characterized by the fact that it is always in movement, always ready to become mobile. Because of the interdependence between psychic agencies, movement in psychoanalysis involves all the mental components and features of the given individual's internal topography. Hence, movement indicates a simultaneous combination of several factors: impulses (the instinctual drive system), tendency (human sexuality in its bisexual dimension), phase (the diphasic nature of sexuality and its deferred aspect, which includes the development of the libidinal system) and development (the temporal dimension of human development from birth to adulthood).

Depending on the various unconscious intrapsychic conflicts, which begin when the psychoanalytic process becomes established and last for the duration of the analysis, these movements have to do with cathexes, stereotypes, and repetition; hence the idea of displacement (of cathexis), of the return of the same (the stereotyped nature of representations), and of repetition of the same, the identical or the similar (as regards action).

Movement may be narcissistic or object-related, and has to do with identification (mimetic, projective or introjective), and with various types of object relations (part- or whole-object; oral, anal, phallic, or genital relationships). It illustrates the development of the drive system via different modalities of projection and introjection (or incorporation, when introjection fails), and it generates two sorts of mental functioning, different and heterogeneous, whose lines of force lie, on the one hand in negation and repression, and, on the other, in denial and splitting. With its ability both to go forward and to turn back, movement, from the point of view of mental functioning, lies at the heart of the problem of regression: the analysis of regression, via the work of interpretation, leads to the lifting of repression, to remembering and consequently to the freeing of affect, representation and insight.

When we speak of change in psychoanalysis, we may be referring to change in meaning (for example, some modification in the meaning of a screen memory) or to change in parameters (for example, the individual's personal myth with respect to elements that sometimes may designate the father, at others the mother, sometimes the primitive level, at others the primary level), or again to change in modes of cathecting (for example, from auto-cathexis to homo- and allo-cathexes, from narcissism to object relations).

If we consider the question from the point of view of the way the mind works, we talk of change in particular when—as a side effect of the work of the analysis—modifications appear in the various metapsychological fields (topographical, dynamic, and economic). These modifications mean that fusion–defusion–re-fusion is no longer subjected in a relentlessly unchanging way to the compulsion to repeat. In this sense, still on the topic of mental functioning, we could say that the connection that apparently comes into operation when movement meets up with change (the effects produced when movement is transformed into change) involves both the mental work linked to the regression–progression pole and that which is controlled by the compulsion to repeat.

Change refers to the outcome of several combined processes and complex movements of fusion–defusion–re-fusion in the course of the analysis, all of them elements that make for transformation in the analysand. These transformations are the fruit of the work done on his or her psychic economy, in connection with modifications in the equilibrium and distribution of the small quantities of energy involved in cathecting and de-cathecting.

It refers also to the effects of the psychoanalytic process, in terms of the analysis of the transference–countertransference situation produced by the minds of patient and analyst working together. It refers, finally, to the dynamic influence of the combination of three factors: the timeless nature of the Unconscious, temporality linked to recalling and processing memories, and the temporality that belongs to the establishment of the setting and the course of the analysis itself.

Thus, change is linked to transformation of the relationship between word-presentations and thing-presentations, to increased flexibility of the cathexes and counter-cathexes of the various topographical agencies ("Where id was, there ego shall be" (Freud, 1933a, p. 80)), to modifications in the economy of the Preconscious–Conscious system, and to better drive and libidinal distribution. When change occurs, it brings in its wake a certain number of subjective modifications.

In addition to contributing to the individual's increased ability to "play" with his or her mental space, (a legacy of the "found/created" (Winnicott, 1967) component used in the interplay with the analyst), change gives greater freedom to fantasy production (extension of the domain of fantasy) and enables heightened awareness, as and when necessary, of movements that lead to and organize repetition, repression or splitting (of the ego or of the object). Each individual retains the ability to modify his or her relationship with the instinctual drives in their interaction with the body, but change allows for transformation in the relationship with our own subjectivity—i.e., with the ability to see our own history in terms of agency, in accordance with the mental history of the internal objects and our links with them—thereby keeping the abundant resources of mental life constantly "at work".

REFERENCES

Anzieu, D. (1959). *L'auto-analyse de Freud et la découverte de la psychanalyse.* Paris: Presses Universitaires de France (1988). *Freud's Self-analysis.* P. Graham (Trans.). New York: International Universities Press, 1986.

Bégoin-Guignard, F. (1984). Adolescence de la féminité. *Adolescence,* 2(2): 221–235.

Bégoin-Guignard, F. (1987). À l'aube du maternel et du féminin. Essai sur deux concepts aussi évidents qu'inconcevables. *Revue française de Psychanalyse, 51*(6): 1491–1503.

Bégoin-Guignard, F. (1988). Le rôle des identifications maternelles et féminines dans le devenir du masculin chez le garçon. *Adolescence,* 6(1): 49–74.

Bergeret, J. (1987). *Les interrogations du psychanalyste.* Paris: Presses Universitaires de France.

Bion, W. R. (1970). *Attention and Interpretation.* London: Tavistock [reprinted London: Karnac, 1984].

Blanchot, M. (1969). *L'entretien infini.* Paris: Gallimard.

Bleger, J. (1967). *Symbiosis and Ambiguity: The Psychoanalysis of Very Early Development.* C. Trollope (Trans.). Columbia University Press (1990).

Blum, H. P. (1974). The borderline childhood of the wolf man. *Journal of the American Psychoanalytical Association, 22*(4): 721–742.

Bokanowski, T. (1979). Présence de Ferenczi dans "Analyse terminée, analyse interminable". *Études Freudiennes, 15–16*: 83–102.

Bokanowski, T. (1981). La trace secrète. *Cahiers Confrontation, 6*: 179–186.

Bokanowski, T. (1989). Le concept de pulsion de mort. Bibliographie critique des auteurs psychanalytiques français. *Revue française de Psychanalyse, 53*(2): 509–534.

Bokanowski, T. (1993). Destins du féminin chez l'homme. *Revue française de Psychanalyse,* Special Congress Edition: 1585–1597.

Bokanowski, T. (1994). Ensuite survient un trouble . . . (Sàndor Ferenczi, le transfert négatif et la dépression de transfert). In: M. Bertrand (Ed.), *Ferenczi, patient et psychanalyste* (pp. 9–52). Paris: L'Harmattan.

Bokanowski, T. (1997). *Sándor Ferenczi.* Paris: Presses Universitaires de France.

Bokanowski, T., & Janin, C. (1994). Le concept de "Nourrisson savant" chez Ferenczi S. (Un échange épistolaire). *Revue française de Psychanalyse, 58*(3): 821–830.

Braunschweig, D., & Fain, M. (1971). *Éros et Antéros.* Paris: Payot.

Braunschweig, D., & Fain, M. (1975). *La nuit, le jour. Essai psychanalytique sur le fonctionnement mental.* Paris: Presses Universitaires de France.

Britton, R. (1989). The missing link: parental sexuality in the Oedipus complex. In: J. Steiner (Ed.), *The Oedipus Complex Today* (pp. 83–102). London: Karnac.

Britton, R. (2004). Subjectivity, objectivity and triangular space. *Psychoanalytic Quarterly, LXXIII*: 47–61.

Cahn, R. (1983). Le procès du cadre ou la passion de Ferenczi. *Revue française de Psychanalyse, 47*(5): 1107–1133.

Caïn, J. (1977). Position et qualité de l'objet dans l'auto-érotisme. *Revue française de Psychanalyse, 41*(5–6): 1009–1017.

Cosnier, J. (1992). L'infantile et la régression. *Revue française de Psychanalyse, 56*(4): 1005–1030.

Cournut, J. (1988). La réaction psychanalytique négative. In: *Parcours du Négatif dans la psychanalyse et la culture* (pp. 26–31): "L'Or d'Atalante". Paris: Champ Vallon.

Cournut, J. (1991). *L'ordinaire de la passion.* Paris: Presses Universitaires de France.

Cournut-Janin, M. & Cournut, J. (1993). La castration et le féminin dans les deux sexes. Report of the 53° CPLFPR. *Revue française de Psychanalyse.* (Special Congress Edition).

Couvreur, C. (1991). Une parole qui porte. *Revue française de Psychanalyse, 55*(3): 611–625.
David, C. (1975). La bisexualité psychique. 35th Congress of Romance Languages Psychoanalysts. *Revue française de Psychanalyse. 39*: 5–6.
David, C. (1984). Un rien qui bouge et tout est changé (à propos de la rencontre). *Nouvelle Revue de Psychanalyse, 30*: 199–213.
David, C. (1992). *La bisexualité psychique. Essais psychanalytiques*. Paris: Payot.
Denis, P. (1997). *Emprise et satisfaction*. Paris: Presses Universitaires de France.
Diatkine, R. (1988). Destins du transfert. *Revue française de Psychanalyse, 52*(4): 803–813.
Diatkine, R. (1993). L'enfant dans l'adulte ou l'éternelle capacité de rêverie. *Revue française de Psychanalyse, 58*(3): 641–648.
Donnet, J.-L. (1985). Sur l'écart théorico-pratique. *Revue française de Psychanalyse, 49*(5): 1289–1305.
Donnet, J.-L. (1995). *Le divan bien tempéré*. Paris: Presses Universitaires de France.
Enriquez, M. (1977). Analyse possible ou impossible. *Topique, 18*: 48–62.
Fain, M. (1987). Psychanalyste, un métier impossible? In: *Les trois métiers impossibles*. 5th Rencontres Psychanalytiques d'Aix-en-Provence (1986). *Confluents psychanalytiques*. Paris: Les Belles Lettres.
Ferenczi, S. (1932). *The Clinical Diary of Sandor Ferenczi*. J. Dupont (Ed.) M. Balint and N.Z. Jackson (Trans.). Cambridge, MA: Harvard University Press, 1988.
Ferenczi, S. (1949). Confusion of tongues between the adult and the child (the language of tenderness and of passion). *International Journal of Psycho-Analysis, 30*: 225–230.
Ferenczi S., & Groddeck G. (1921–1933). *The Ferenczi–Groddeck Correspondence (1921–1933)*. Edited & annotated by C. Fortune. New York: Other Press, 2002.
Ferenczi, S., & Rank, O. (1924). *The Development of Psychoanalysis*. London: Karnac, 1986.
Freud, S. (1900a). *The Interpretation of Dreams. S.E., 4–5*. London: Hogarth.
Freud, S. (1905d). *Three Essays on the Theory of Sexuality. S.E., 7*: 125–245. London: Hogarth.
Freud, S. (1905e). Fragment of an analysis of a case of hysteria. *S.E., 7*: 3–122. London: Hogarth.
Freud, S. (1909d). Notes upon a case of obsessional neurosis. *S.E., 10*: 155–249. London: Hogarth.

Freud, S. (1910c). *Leonardo da Vinci and a Memory of his Childhood. S.E., 11*, 59–137. London: Hogarth.
Freud, S. (1911b). Formulations on the two principles of mental functioning. *S.E., 12*: 215–226. London: Hogarth.
Freud, S. (1911c). Psycho-analytic notes on an autobiographical account of a case of paranoia (dementia paranoides). *S.E., 12*: 3–82. London: Hogarth.
Freud, S. (1912b). The dynamics of transference. *S.E., 12*: 99–108. London: Hogarth.
Freud, S. (1914g). Remembering, repeating and working-through (Further recommendations on the technique of psycho-analysis, II). *S.E., 12*: 147–156. London: Hogarth.
Freud, S. (1917c). On transformations of instinct as exemplified in anal erotism. *S.E., 17*: 127–133. London: Hogarth.
Freud, S. (1918b). From the history of an infantile neurosis. *S.E., 17*: 3–122. London: Hogarth.
Freud, S. (1919e). A child is being beaten. *S.E., 17*: 177–204. London: Hogarth.
Freud, S. (1920a). The psychogenesis of a case of female homosexuality. *S.E., 18*: 147–172. London: Hogarth.
Freud, S. (1920g). *Beyond the Pleasure Principle*. London, 1961. *S.E., 18*: 7–64. London: Hogarth.
Freud, S. (1923a). Two encyclopaedia articles. *S.E., 18*: 235–259. London: Hogarth.
Freud, S. (1923b). *The Ego and the Id. S.E., 19*: 3–66. London: Hogarth.
Freud, S. (1923d). A seventeenth-century demonological neurosis. *S.E., 19*: 69–105. London: Hogarth.
Freud, S. (1924c). The economic problem of masochism. *S.E., 19*, 157–170. London: Hogarth.
Freud, S. (1926e). *The Question of Lay Analysis. S.E., 20*, 179–258. London: Hogarth.
Freud, S. (1928b). Dostoevsky and parricide. *S.E., 21*: 175–194. London: Hogarth.
Freud, S. (1933a (1932)). *New Introductory Lectures on Psycho-Analysis. S.E., 22*: 3–182. London: Hogarth.
Freud, S. (1936a). A disturbance of memory on the Acropolis. *S.E., 22*: 239–248. London: Hogarth.
Freud, S. (1937c). Analysis terminable and interminable. *S.E., 23*: 211–253. London: Hogarth.
Freud, S. (1937d). Constructions in analysis. *S.E., 23*: 257–269. London: Hogarth.

Freud, S. (1939a). Moses and monotheism: three essays. *S.E.*, *23*: 3–137. London: Hogarth.

Freud, S. (1940a). An outline of psychoanalysis. *S. E.*, *23*: 141–207. London: Hogarth.

Freud, S. (1950a). A project for a scientific psychology. In: *The Origins of Psycho-Analysis. S.E.*, *1*: 283–397.

Freud, S. (1963a)[1909–1939]. *Psycho-Analysis and Faith. The Letters of Sigmund Freud and Oskar Pfister.* H. Meng & E. L. Freud (Eds.), E. Mosbacher (Trans.). London and New York.

Freud, S., & Breuer, J. (1895d). *Studies on Hysteria. S.E.*, 2. London: Hogarth.

Freud, S., & Ferenczi S. (1994). *The Correspondence of Sigmund Freud and Sandor Ferenczi: 1908–1914.* Cambridge, MA: Belknap Press.

Freud, S., & Ferenczi S. (1996). *The Correspondence of Sigmund Freud and Sandor Ferenczi: 1914–1919.* Cambridge, MA: Belknap Press.

Gantheret, F. (1988). Habemus papam! *Nouvelle Revue de Psychanalyse*, *38*: 47–72.

Gibeault, A. (1992). Marc ou le parcours du combattant. Des conditions de la régression dans la cure. *Revue française de Psychanalyse*, *56*(4): 978–994.

Gillibert, J. (1977). De l'autoérotisme. Report of the 37th Congress of Romance Languages Psychoanalysts. *Revue française de Psychanalyse*, *41*: 5–6.

Gillibert, J. (1979). *L'OEdipe maniaque* 3. Paris: Payot.

Goethe, J. W. von (1874). *Poems.* E. A. Bowring (Trans.). New York: Thomas Y. Crowell.

Green, A. (1973). Le genre neutre. *Nouvelle Revue de Psychanalyse*, *7*: 251–262.

Green, A. (1975). La sexualisation et son économie. In: *Propédeutique (La métapsychologie revisitée)* (pp. 51–68). "L'Or d'Atalante". Paris: Champ Vallon, 1995.

Green, A. (1983). *Narcissisme de vie, narcissisme de mort.* Paris: Les Éditions de Minuit. English edition: *Life Narcissism, Death Narcissism.* A. Weller (Trans.). London: Free Association, 2001.

Green, A. (1986a). Féminité et masculinité (à propos de la conférence de F. Bégoin-Guignard). *Bulletin de la Société Psychanalytique de Paris. 9*: 21–30.

Green, A. (1986b). Pulsion de mort, narcissisme négatif, fonction désobjectalisante. In: *La pulsion de mort* (pp. 49–59). First Symposium of the European Federation of Psychoanalysis (Marseille, 1984). Paris: Presses Universitaires de France.

Green, A. (1990). *La folie privée*. Paris: Gallimard. English edition: *On Private Madness*. London: Karnac, 1996.

Green, A. (1993a). "L'analité primaire dans la relation anale". In *La névrose obsessionnelle. Monographie de la Revue française de Psychanalyse* (pp. 61–86). Paris: Presses Universitaires de France.

Green, A. (1993b). *Le travail du négatif*. Paris: Les Éditions de Minuit. (*The Work of the Negative*, A. Weller (Trans.). London: Free Association, 1999.

Guignard, F. (1993). L'enfant dans le psychanalyste. *Revue française de Psychanalyse, 58*(3): 649–659.

Guignard, F. (1996). *Au vif de l'infantile*. Lausanne: Delachaux et Niestlé.

Guignard, F. (1997). *Épître à l'Objet*. Paris: Presses Universitaires de France.

Guillaumin, J. (1987). *Entre blessure et cicatrice. Le destin du négatif dans la psychanalyse.* "L'Or d'Atalante". Paris: Champ Vallon.

Janin, C. (1996). *Figures et destin du traumatisme*. Paris: Presses Universitaires de France.

Kaës, R. (1989). Le pacte dénégatif dans les ensembles transsubjectifs. In: *Le négatif. Figures et modalités* (pp. 101–136). Paris: Dunod.

Kestemberg, E. (1984). "Astrid" ou homosexualité, identité, adolescence. Quelques propositions hypothétiques. *Cahiers du Centre de Psychanalyse et de Psychothérapie, 8*: 1–30.

King, P., & Steiner, R. (Eds.) (1992). *The Freud–Klein Controversies, 1941–1945*. London: Karnac.

Klein, M. (1932). *The Psycho-Analysis of Children. The Writings of Melanie Klein*, vol. II. London: The Hogarth Press and the Institute of Psycho-Analysis, 1986.

Lacan, J. (1964). *Le Séminaire, Livre XI*. J.-A. Miller (Ed.). Paris: Le Seuil, 1973. *The Seminar of Jacques Lacan, Book XI: The Four Fundamental Concepts of Psychoanalysis*. New York: Norton, 1998.

Laplanche, J., & Pontalis, J.-B. (1967). *Vocabulaire de la Psychanalyse*. Paris: Presses Universitaires de France. *The Language of Psychoanalysis*, D. Nicholson-Smith (Trans.). London: Hogarth, 1973 [reprinted London: Karnac, 1988].

Le Guen, C. (1989). *La dialectique freudienne—II Théorie de la méthode psychanalytique*. Paris: Presses Universitaires de France.

M'Uzan, M. de (1969). Le même et l'identique. In: *De l'art à la mort*. Paris: Gallimard, 1977.

M'Uzan, M. de (1988). Stratégie et tactique à propos des interprétations freudiennes et kleiniennes. *Revue française de Psychanalyse, 52*(3): 657–663.

Marinov, V. (1990). *Figures du crime chez Dostoièvski*. Paris: Presses Universitaires de France.

Masson, J. M. (Ed.) (1985). *The Complete Letters of Sigmund Freud to Wilhelm Fliess, 1887–1904*. Cambridge, MA: Harvard University Press.

McDougall, J. (1982). *Théâtre du Je*. Paris: Gallimard. English translation: *Theatres of the Mind: Illusion and Truth on the Psychoanalytic Stage*. London: Free Association, 1986.

Neyraut, M. (1974). *Le transfert*. Paris: Presses Universitaires de France.

Pasche, F. (1974). Le passé recomposé. *Revue française de Psychanalyse, 38*(2–3): 171–196.

Reik, T. (1940). *From Thirty Years with Freud*. R. Winston (Trans.). New York: International Universities Press.

Rosenberg, B. (1982). Masochisme mortifère et masochisme gardien de la vie. *Monographies de la Revue française de Psychanalyse*. Paris: Presses Universitaires de France, 1991.

Rosolato, G. (1978). *La relation d'inconnu*. Paris: Gallimard.

Schaeffer, J. (1997). *Le refus du féminin*. Paris: Presses Universitaires de France.

Stein, C. (1971). *L'enfant imaginaire*. Paris: Denoël.

Urtubey L. de (1983). *Freud et le diable*. Paris: Presses Universitaires de France.

Urtubey, L. de (1994). Le travail de contre-transfert. Report of the 54° CPLFPR *Revue française de Psychanalyse, 58* (Special Congress Edition): 1271–1372.

Viderman, S. (1970). *La construction de l'espace analytique*. Paris: Denoël.

Viderman, S. (1974). La bouteille à la mer. *Revue française de Psychanalyse, 38*(2–3): 323–384.

Viderman, S. (1977). *Le céleste et le sublunaire*. Paris: Presses Universitaires de France.

Winnicott, D. W. (1962). A personal view of the Kleinian contribution. In: *The Maturational Processes and the Facilitating Environment. Studies in the Theory of Emotional Development*. London: Hogarth, 1965.

Winnicott, D. W. (1963). On communication. In: *The Maturational Processes and the Facilitating Environment. Studies in the Theory of Emotional Development*. London: Hogarth, 1965.

Winnicott, D. W. (1966). The split-off male and female elements to be found in men and women. In: C. Winnicott, R. Shepherd, & M. Davis (Eds.), Winnicott, D. W. (1989), *Psycho-analytic Explorations* . London: Karnac.

Winnicott, D. W. (1967). The location of cultural experience. *International Journal of Psycho-Analysis, 48*: 368–372.

Winnicott, D. W. (1971). *Playing and Reality*. London: Tavistock.

Winnicott, D. W. (1987). *The Spontaneous Gesture. Selected Letters of D. W. Winnicott*. F. Rodman (Ed.). Cambridge, MA: Harvard University Press.

INDEX